ESP | CURRICULUM GUIDE

by R. A. McConnell

RESEARCH PROFESSOR OF BIOPHYSICS

Department of Biophysics and Microbiology
University of Pittsburgh, Pennsylvania

SIMON AND SCHUSTER | NEW YORK

SECOND PRINTING

SBN 671-21007-6 Casebound edition
SBN 671-21009-2 Fireside paperback edition
Library of Congress Catalog Card Number: 75–159134
Designed by Irving Perkins
Manufactured in the United States of America

CONTENTS

PREFACE

Although the fact is unknown to most educators, extrasensory perception is receiving increasing but still limited attention in textbooks of general psychology at both high school and college levels.

In our present state of little knowledge it appears that the principal values to be gained by a student who is not going to devote a large amount of time or effort to the subject will be a deepened understanding of scientific method and a renewed sense of wonder toward man and his potentialities. I believe these are among the values essential to a recovery of social morality, and this explains why I think the disciplined study of ESP can be of importance today.

As one of a small group of university scientists actively engaged in research on ESP, I want to give as many teachers as possible whatever help I can, so that they may teach this subject in an honest, accurate, and exciting way. For that reason I have prepared this curriculum guide as a supplementary source of information for those who care to use it.

Recognizing that the most significant aspects of a pioneering science are often conveyed in the outlook of the investigators, I have not tried to avoid expressions of personal attitude where these seemed appropriate to my purpose.

I ‖ HOW THIS PRESENTATION IS ORGANIZED

This curriculum guide is for secondary-school and college teachers of psychology, biology, and general science who may wish to teach extra-sensory perception and related topics, either briefly or as a formal course unit, or who may have occasion to recommend the purchase of library materials for student projects on this subject. The instructor who has only limited time should turn first to the Syllabus to see what can be done in the classroom.

The educational challenge of ESP lies in four topical areas: in the use of scientific method, in the nature of scientific controversy, in the unknown psychological conditions necessary for the production of ESP, and in its philosophic implications.

The presentation and development of these topics in your class will require certain starting information, which this curriculum guide provides as indicated in the table of contents. Attention is called to the comments offered after each item under "Books and Articles Recommended." These are an important part of what you need to know.

I have rejected one commonly used approach to parapsychology, namely, through mathematical statistics. The "binomial distribution" might be studied by having every student in the class throw a coin or a die 500 times. This could lead to the idea of the "null hypothesis." The same method could then be applied to an ESP card-guessing experiment.

The disadvantage of the statistical approach is that it places emphasis where it does not belong. Statistical method, although commonly used in this research, is merely a tool made necessary by the fact that in most ESP experiments the effects are too weak to be recognized by inspection.

In order to evaluate any experiment done in your class it may be necessary to make a probability determination, and this, in turn, will require explaining "probability" and "null hypothesis" if these concepts have not previously been covered. My recommendation is that the time for this be minimized. It would be regrettable if the student were allowed to acquire a misconception about ESP that is common among scientists, namely, that ESP research is a matter of routinized card guessing plus elementary probability theory.

I shall be grateful if those who use this curriculum guide will send me their criticisms and suggestions as outlined in Appendix 7.

II | IMPORTANT IDEAS OF SCIENCE ILLUSTRATED BY ESP

What is to be learned about science in general from the study of ESP? Here are some ideas that seem important to me. You may find others to add to the list.

The two essential features of scientific method are theory and experiment.

In its first stage of development a new field of science is usually unscientific or even antiscientific, as in the case of alchemy, which evolved into chemistry.

Scientists welcome minor changes in their thinking but vigorously oppose major changes.

The wide acceptance of a revolutionary scientific idea will depend primarily upon philosophic beliefs or practical applications, but scarcely at all upon laboratory evidence.

In science, as in every area of human endeavor, the fact that a man has achieved an outstanding reputation does not mean that all of his opinions are correct.

The research problems one can undertake in a field of science seem limitless, but are restricted as a practical matter by present understanding and technique, upon which we must build.

Revolutionary scientific research is often slow and unexciting, requiring painstaking attention to detail.

Worthwhile research does not necessarily require expensive tools.

To avoid wasting time, before beginning scientific research of any kind, one must study what other people have done in the same area.

No matter how well intended they may be, descriptions of one person's experiment by another are usually misleading. One must go to the original research report to make a definitive evaluation.

In a scientific sense, we do not know what man is. Our ideas about how man relates to man and to the rest of the universe are too primitive and fragmentary to allow us to distinguish between moral values that are compatible with reality and those that are not.

III
BOOKS AND ARTICLES RECOMMENDED FOR THE SCHOOL LIBRARY, WITH A COMMENTARY ON EACH ITEM

(*Book prices of 1971 are given.*)

Anderson, M. L., and R. A. McConnell. "Fantasy Testing for ESP in a Fourth- and Fifth-Grade Class," *Journal of Psychology,* LII (1961), 491–503.

The references at the end of this paper lead backward to a long series of experiments by M. L. Anderson, R. White, J. G. Van Busschbach, and others on classroom testing for ESP, mostly in the elementary grades. These papers raise significant questions about the possible importance of student-teacher ESP relationships in the teaching process.

Anderson and McConnell have exhausted their supply of reprints, but the *Journal of Psychology* can be found in any university or public library serving serious psychological research.

Gudas, F., ed. *Extrasensory Perception*
CHARLES SCRIBNER'S SONS
597 FIFTH AVENUE
NEW YORK, N.Y. 10017
(Copyright 1961; paperback, $2.95)

This is a scholarly anthology of writings on the question of ESP, stretching from Francis Bacon through Michael Faraday, Mark Twain, and J. B. Rhine to B. F. Skinner. It establishes a historical, philosophic, and methodological perspective. Many of its 23 authors are men of eminence; all are professionally respectable. Their writings include various extremes of intelligent (but not necessarily correctly reasoned) opinion on the subject of psi phenomena. (The Greek letter *psi* [silent *p*, long *i*] is now used interchangeably with the older words "psychic" and "psychical" to designate extrasensory perception, psychokinesis, and related effects.)

Since the book does not deal directly with the experimental evidence, it will not enable the reader to decide whether ESP is real. By its diversity it may encourage the superficial student to adopt a dilettante agnosticism. To the more thoughtful it will reveal *why* there is an ESP controversy on what is ostensibly simply a question of experimental fact. It offers subtle lessons on the difficulty of communicating by language, whether across centuries or between professions.

This work may seem too sophisticated for high school students or even for the college freshmen, to whom, as a "Scribner Research Anthology," it is directed. But in an age when children are asking to be treated as adults, it is essential that teachers permit them to test the range of their comprehension.

The superior student may be able to meet the challenge of the book as a whole. As required reading for the class I suggest the twelve-page selection from William James's *The Will to Believe,* written at the end of the nineteenth century. James has often been called America's greatest psychologist. In this excerpt he displays the timelessness of the thoughts of a wise man, while in gracious prose he tells a little of the early history of the Society for Psychical Research,* and along the way explains how he became personally convinced of the reality of ESP.

The James excerpt will provide a needed historical background; for I suspect that in the classroom of the average course unit on ESP there will be no time for history as such.

Heywood, R. *Beyond the Reach of Sense: An Inquiry into Extrasensory Perception*

E. P. DUTTON & COMPANY, INC.

201 PARK AVENUE SOUTH

NEW YORK, N.Y. 10003

(Copyright 1959; 1961 edition, $4.95. Published in England under the title *The Sixth Sense*.)

---

* The Society for Psychical Research, of London, has a very remarkable early history, numbering among its officers, for example, people whose names today are still among the most illustrious in the field of physics. This society is one of three international-membership, English-language organizations devoted to psychical research. Another is the American Society for Psychical Research, which began as an offshoot of the London S.P.R. but is now fully independent. Both of these organizations publish journals and offer membership to all who are interested. The Parapsychological Association was founded as a professional society in 1957 to meet the growing needs of trained specialists in psychical research. Its constitutional objectives are "to advance parapsychology as a science, to disseminate knowledge of the field, and to integrate the findings with those of other branches of science." There is close cooperation among all three organizations.

The author, a child of our century's childhood, is not a scientist but a well-educated and widely traveled upper-class Englishwoman of unusual energy, intelligence, and independence. She is also a "psychic" (see her autobiography, below).

For these reasons she came to know almost everyone who has been important in the Society for Psychical Research in the last several decades. Her book supplements that of Murphy and Dale (described below) by emphasizing the English research and by providing a more genial review of the literature. Because it is informal and yet reasonably authoritative, this book, better than any other in print and known to me, allows one easily to get a feeling for the tremendous scope of the field of parapsychology.

As required student reading I suggest Chapters 1 and 2—believing that few will be able to stop before finishing Chapter 6. These early chapters include a beautifully written introduction to the ideas of the field and a capsule history of ESP from ancient times through the early days of the Society for Psychical Research.

Chapters 7–13 describe psychic "mediumship" of various kinds. The subject becomes tedious, and the beginner may wish to skim— perhaps reading in full, out of curiosity, Chapter 11, on "Patience Worth." (She is a literary "Bridey Murphy," discovered in Missouri in the early twentieth century.) Much of the material of these chapters is more readably given in Chapter 7 of Murphy and Dale's *Challenge of Psychical Research* (see below). Heywood's version, on the other hand, is pleasingly decorated with information about the familial and professional interrelationships among the eminent members of the Society for Psychical Research.

Whether formally or informally presented to us, the mediums have the same message: Studying psi as it appears in these gifted psychics could be compared to trying to understand a complex chemical reaction three centuries ago, before the atomic nature of the elements was known. Our need today is for simple, controlled experiments —if such are possible in parapsychology.

Chapters 14–16 sketch lightly the history of experimental parapsychology prior to about 1950, with emphasis on the struggles and achievements of the English workers. To readers familiar only with American research the extent of this early evidence may come as a surprise. How many times, in how many places, must an experiment be repeated before other scientists will consider it worthy of attention? One is reminded of the ancient Greek myth in which Sisyphus, King of Corinth, having revealed information about Zeus, was doomed forever to push a rock uphill only to have it roll to the bottom again.

Four book appendices outline tentative theories about psychic phenomena by various people. The last appendix describes the thinking of C. D. Broad (Cambridge) and H. H. Price (Oxford), who are among the most eminent of living classical philosophers. In fourteen pages one can sample (partly at second hand) what many regard as the most sophisticated thinking yet done on the possible meaning of ESP. From these pages, as much as from the bizarre nature of spontaneous psi, the student can understand why established scientists fear the entire field of ESP.

In the near future of our civilization, great intellectual courage will be needed to explore further this neglected area of reality and to fit it into our everyday philosophy. Our youth have that courage—if only they will lay aside the enjoyment of their sincerity, and discipline themselves to search for fuller understanding.

From this book one comes to appreciate the complexity of parapsychological phenomena and to accept the fact that extensive preparation is needed by anyone who wishes to enter the field as an independent professional investigator.

Heywood, R. *ESP: A Personal Memoir*
E. P. DUTTON & COMPANY, INC.
201 PARK AVENUE SOUTH
NEW YORK, N.Y. 10003
(Copyright 1964; $5.95. Published in England under the title *The Infinite Hive: A Personal Record of Extrasensory Experiences*.)

Many of us have a little ESP; a few people have a lot. The quality of spontaneous psychic manifestations among ordinary people can be understood from L. E. Rhine's *Hidden Channels of the Mind* (see pp. 27–28). The quasi-spontaneous psychic productions of exceptionally psychic individuals while trying to demonstrate or explore their abilities are described in R. Heywood's *Beyond the Reach of Sense* and in Murphy and Dale's *Challenge of Psychical Research*. But what is it like to *be* an exceptionally psychic person? And specifically, what is the outcome when a member of the ruling elite of a Western country is born with outstanding psi abilities plus the determination to live a normal life? This second book by Mrs. Heywood is the autobiography of such a person—written reluctantly and out of a sense of obligation to science.

No normal, reasonable person can read this book for the first time without disbelief. If the other works of this bibliography are thoughtfully studied over a period of time, disbelief of Heywood's story may turn into comprehension of the individuality of human beings. We are wildly diverse, not only in our body structures (as every surgeon knows) but also in the potentialities of our minds.

A word of caution may be helpful. Except for the emergence "by ESP" of publicly verifiable information, Mrs. Heywood's psychic experiences are all subjective. In describing them for us she is limited by our language, but that is not the important point. When she hears "singing" (in a manner roughly analogous to the way many mediums see "auras") it is not to be thought of as in any way a normal hearing process using the ear, but only as a probably trivial involvement of the hearing-perception mechanism in the brain itself. In an earlier time she would have been called insane or a witch. Her books show

that she is in good touch with everyday reality—
better than most of us. Scientifically, we are at a
loss in trying to interpret her additional, bizarre,
subjective experiences. Small wonder that when
similar things have been written by less intelligent psychics, scientists have reacted unfavor-
ably and the entire field has gained a bad name.

Murphy, G., and L. Dale. *Challenge of Psychical
Research*

HARPER & ROW, INC.

49 E. 33 STREET

NEW YORK, N.Y. 10016

(Copyright 1961; clothbound, $6.50, paper-
back, $1.95)

Dr. Murphy, a distinguished psychologist, has
been president of the American Psychological
Association and of both the American Society
and the (London) Society for Psychical Research. His feet are thus firmly planted, one in
orthodoxy and one in heresy. Mrs. Dale has for
several decades been a vitalizing force in the
American Society for Psychical Research.

This book gives excerpts and abstracts from
the literature of the best known evidence for
ESP and related effects, plus extensive critical
comment of a fairly general kind. It covers spontaneous cases of ESP, experimental ESP and
psychokinesis, and, from an evidential point of
view, the question of whether some part of
human personality might survive after bodily
death.

Pratt, J. G., J. B. Rhine, B. M. Smith, C. E. Stuart, and J. A. Greenwood. *Extrasensory Perception After Sixty Years*

BRUCE HUMPHRIES, PUBS.

BOX 111

68 BEACON STREET

SOMERVILLE, MASS. 02143

(Copyright 1940; reprinted 1966; $5.95)

This landmark in the history of parapsychology might instead have been titled *An Encyclopedia of Experimental ESP*. Until there is a definitive study of the origins of parapsychology, Chapter 1 will remain a helpful guide to the pre-experimental era. The next five chapters survey in detail the ESP methods, experiments, and criticisms in the period 1882–1940. A later section tells what was known of the nature of the ESP process. There are 16 appendices with still useful statistical procedures and tables. The leading critics of 1940 were invited to read the evidential chapters and to have their criticism published therewith as submitted.

At the time the book was written there were 145 experimental reports to review. Since then there have been over 1,000 parapsychological publications abstracted in *Psychological Abstracts* (published by the American Psychological Association) —750 of these since 1950. Perhaps half of the abstracts covered strictly experimental reports and thus are comparable to the 145 available up to 1940.

The effect of this continually growing stream

of papers has been to erode disbelief in ESP until most psychologists are no longer willing publicly to deny the evidence for the phenomenon. A more typical position today is that "ESP may occur, but the effect is too small to be of any importance to society." To this the best reply may be that the raising of a pith ball by rubbed amber was a trivial phenomenon known for at least 2,000 years before it was seriously investigated and found to be of some importance.

Rhine, J. B. *Extrasensory Perception*
BRUCE HUMPHRIES, PUBS.
BOX 111
68 BEACON STREET
SOMERVILLE, MASS. 02143
(First publication, 1934; reprinted, 1964; paperback, $2.95.)

With this book Dr. Joseph Banks Rhine started "the ESP controversy." What was it in his work that called forth from scientists an angry public response to a subject hitherto ignored?

Although serious psychical research began in 1882, until 1934 most educated people assumed that "telepathy" and "clairvoyance" were superstition. For these words Rhine introduced a more scientific-sounding term, "extrasensory perception," and the field as a whole he called "parapsychology." This linguistic bid for respectability was doubtless effective with some readers—and perhaps annoyed others.

In later writing Rhine offended skeptics by

philosophic speculation about the importance of ESP, but this first book is almost entirely a statement of the experimental results obtained by himself and by those who preceded him. I am inclined to think that the matter-of-factness of his presentation was a major, successful tactic in his plan to attract attention.

In his second chapter, reviewing the work of others, Rhine specifically acknowledged that ESP was an *experimentally* established fact, "amply proved, over and over," before he came on the stage (p. 25). This makes it all the more interesting that he was the first to have succeeded in noticeably arousing the scientific world.

What impressed his readers most, I think, was the seeming ease with which he achieved his miraculous results. In three years he found eight college students who, in more than 60,000 card guesses made under a wide variety of conditions, achieved an average number of successes more than 50 percent greater than the expected chance average. In many instances, near-perfect scores were reported with the use of card decks in which the probability of a chance success was one in five. Admittedly, all of Rhine's subjects showed a "decline effect," but for the most part this occurred only over a period of many months. To those who understood statistics it sounded as though, if one wanted to walk on water every day at 4 o'clock, all one needed was a deck of cards and a willingness to try.

Many did try—but succeeded only in confirming the laws of probability. A very few scientists elsewhere were able to produce spectacular results comparable to Rhine's, but usually of more limited duration. They, like Rhine, were called self-deceivers or worse. Orthodoxy, apparently vindicated, wanted to hear no more about ESP.

Although Rhine continued his work successfully on a more modest scale, neither he nor his slowly growing list of followers, scattered over the earth, ever succeeded in recreating the easy magic that happened in 1931–33 at Durham, North Carolina.

Now, some twoscore years later, when Rhine's experiments have become a very minor part of the total evidence for ESP, parapsychologists are still puzzled as to how he did it. We know that enthusiasm is not enough. Perhaps there was something in Rhine's personality akin to the "charisma" of great leaders in politics and religion. Having myself worked very hard to produce rigorously controlled but rather modest evidence for psychic phenomena, I must confess that the history of the research of that period stirs in me a little of the same awe and disbelief that I feel toward the Italian Renaissance.

There is one more peculiar aspect of Rhine's early work that helps explain the attention he attracted. His mathematical methods, although adequate for his purpose, were only approximate and were a few years out of date. His data-gathering procedures were called "sloppy" by his critics—although history is more likely to say the methods were appropriate to the psychological nature of the phenomenon and good enough to establish, independently of all preceding research, a strong, *prima facie* case for ESP. Be that as it may, these apparent technical weaknesses were important for the success of the book in the following way.

We may dislike an idea intensely, but unless we think we can destroy it by argument, we prefer to ignore it. In view of the "silent treatment" given to the many subsequent, more nearly perfect ESP experiments done by Rhine and others, it appears fortunate for the advancement of truth that the disbelieving scientists of the 1930s were trapped by his seeming vulnerability into counterattacking this heretic from Duke University. Were these flaws in Rhine's work intentional or were they accidental? You may decide this for yourself when you read the book.

Lest we think that the ESP controversy is ended, I will cite a recent incident that seems to support the thesis that, when an idea offends us, we try to destroy it by argument; and when that fails, we try to ignore it; and when that is no longer possible, we hope to suppress it by violence.

An eminent nuclear physicist, a member of the National Academy of Sciences, a past president of the American Physical Society and of the American Association for the Advancement of Science, a former director of the National Bureau of Standards, and currently a professor at the University of Colorado—these are the credentials of Dr. E. U. Condon.

Those over thirty may remember Dr. Condon as a scientist-martyr of the McCarthy era, who lost his government security clearance for access to secret research in 1954 and had to change his employment because of his liberal political views.

More recently Dr. Condon has been in the news (*Science*, CLXI, July 26, 1968, 339–342) as the director of a U.S. Air Force project on which $500,000 was spent to investigate the reality of "flying saucers," a phenomenon for which no laboratory evidence whatsoever exists. (Unfortunately, no government money has ever been given to a formal investigation of the claims for ESP and psychokinesis.)

On April 26, 1969, in a speech before the American Philosophical Society at Philadelphia, as subsequently released by him to the press and as printed in the intellectually oriented *Bulletin of the Atomic Scientists* for science and public affairs (December 1969, pp. 6–8) the following passages appeared—offered here without comment:

> Flying saucers and astrology are not the only pseudo-sciences which have a considerable following among us. There used to be spiritualism, there continues to be extrasensory perception, psychokinesis, and a host of others. . . . Where corruption of children's minds is at stake, I do not believe in freedom of the press or freedom of speech. In my view, publishers who publish or teachers who teach any of the pseudo-sciences as established truth should, on

being found guilty, be publicly horsewhipped, and forever banned from further activity in these usually honorable professions.

We should not suppose, however, that science never moves forward. At Boston, Massachusetts, on December 30, 1969, by a vote of approximately 165 to 30, the Council of the American Association for the Advancement of Science accepted the Parapsychological Association as an "affiliated society." The Parapsychological Association, founded in 1957, with a current total membership of about 200, includes almost all professionally qualified parapsychologists in non-Communist countries the world over.

Rhine, Louisa E. *Hidden Channels of the Mind*
APOLLO EDITIONS, INC.
201 PARK AVENUE SOUTH
NEW YORK, N.Y. 10003
(Copyright 1961; 1966 paperback edition, $2.45)

Dr. Louisa Rhine is the wife of Dr. J. B. Rhine, the man who has done most to advance the cause of parapsychology in our time.

This book for the layman summarizes a serious survey of spontaneous ESP. The examples given are not offered as evidence for the reality of the phenomenon—"proof" is a task for the laboratory —but were selected to illustrate the characteristics of ESP found repeatedly in a collection of several thousand probably authentic cases.

In a quasi-systematic fashion the author discusses variables (such as distance, time, sex, and age) , modes of expression (dreams, visions, intuitions) , range of ESP subject matter, accuracy, recognizability, and the tendency of individuals to exhibit ESP only in the limited ways presumably appropriate to their personalities.

After a pleasant trip through this book the reader will have acquired an accurate feeling for the range of ESP experienced in everyday life by more or less ordinary people. In a large measure the findings of this book have been confirmed, or as the case may be, not disconfirmed, by the laboratory research of ESP.

Rhine, Louisa E. *Mind over Matter, Psychokinesis*

THE MACMILLAN COMPANY
866 THIRD AVENUE
NEW YORK, N.Y. 10022
(Copyright, 1970; $7.95)

Here is a popular, noncritical, comprehensive review of all modern psychokinetic experiments published prior to the end of 1968.* It is the only such summary available. Although it ought not to convince anyone of the reality of PK, it deserves our approbation. With a task so difficult, who among us could have done better?

Mrs. Rhine's ideas as to "what might be expected on the basis of physical principles" will seem naïve to most physicists. And her *ad hoc*

---

* For a typical experiment see p. 56 of this curriculum guide.

speculations about psychological mechanisms, although plausible and stimulating, are not necessarily correct.

From her book, truthful impressions may be gained as to the massiveness of the PK literature, the futility of seeking the acceptance of scientists by gathering laboratory data, the pervasiveness of the "scoring-decline effect," the seeming perversity of the PK phenomenon, and the importance and timeliness of an effort to sweep up all the clutter from our laboratories and take it out into the fresh air of life for casual inspection.

For the open-minded nonspecialist I recommend Chapter 1 and the first half of Chapter 2 as necessary background, plus Chapters 12, 13, and 14 as the heart of the book. The do-or-die skeptic should speed-read the entire work, with emphasis on Chapter 12, so that he can grasp the scope of the evidence with which he must deal when he turns to the journals. Parapsychologists will find in this book as a whole a much-needed guide to the literature.

Chapters 1 and 5 include a brief history of the founding and evolution of the Rhine laboratory at Duke University.

The first part of Chapter 2 conveys a correct feeling for the kind of experimenter attitude that has proved most successful in producing PK and ESP.

Chapter 3 tells the story of the discovery of the tendency of PK success to die away in progressing from the beginning to the end of each cluster of data, and how this made it possible to find good evidence for PK in most of the early experiments, which were of otherwise doubtful value.

Chapters 4 through 11 review 81 papers by 52 authors. Dr. Rhine's objective is to explore the nature of PK rather than to prove its occurrence. Nevertheless the warning must be given that most of these experiments would be rejected as significant evidence for PK by any competent scientist studying the original papers. In many instances the experimental procedures were defective. In all but a few papers the reporting is inadequate. For the most part the qualifications of the experimenters are unknown.

This is not a criticism of the original journal editors, who have published the best of what was offered, or of the experimenters, whose valiant efforts are not without scientific importance. Rather, the variable quality of these papers reflects the elusiveness of PK, the pretheoretical state of our knowledge, and the neglect of this field by those best qualified to explore it.

Chapter 12, devoted to the "cube-placement" research done by Haakon Forwald, is outstanding in several respects. Using himself as the test subject, Forwald, a Swedish electrical engineer, has done more PK experiments over a longer period of time than anyone else. Since 1950, in his tireless efforts to find the physical parameters of success, he has clearly established the psychological character of the PK process and has convincingly exhibited his own empirical orientation toward the problem.

Chapter 13 deals with the possibility of using PK in gambling, with claims that photographic film can be blackened by PK, and with the sketchy available evidence that the growth of fungi, plants, one-celled organisms, and even mouse tissue might be affected by "wishing."

Chapter 14 describes evidence for the spontaneous occurrence of PK in everyday life, in both recurrent and nonrecurrent forms. Included here are the questions of house hauntings and the purported self-moving of objects near people in great emotional stress.

The last chapter is devoted to the possible relation of PK to the rest of knowledge. If the chapter says little, it is because it is too soon for much to be said. In broad outline, the most reasonable explanatory proposal for psi phenomena is that a personal mind entity relates with the human body through the intermediation of the brain neurons, and that both spontaneous and laboratory PK and ESP are reciprocal leakage effects outside the normal evolutionary channel.

The most eminent of those proposing this theory is Sir John Eccles, Nobel prizewinner in neurophysiology. In 1953 he devoted to these ideas the last chapter of his otherwise orthodox text, *The Neurophysiological Basis of Mind.*

Eccles is not the first Nobel prizewinner to offer encouragement to parapsychological research. Lord Rayleigh, the giant of classical physics, accepted the presidency of the Society for Psychical Research in 1919 after having been a member since shortly after its founding in 1882.

His successor at Cambridge University, Sir J. J. Thomson, who built the Cavendish Laboratory into a world center of atomic physics and who received a Nobel Prize in 1906, was a member of the governing council or a vice-president of the Society for Psychical Research for 53 years.

Nobel laureate Charles Richet, the French physiologist, described his experiments in ESP in a 1923 book titled *Thirty Years of Psychical Research* (*Traité de Métapsychique,* 1922).

Such, however, is the nature of human belief (among scientists as well as ordinary mortals) that neither scientific eminence nor laboratory evidence can successfully oppose the spirit of the time. Many years have passed, and it is our good fortune now to have at last reached the stage when parapsychology is receiving official recognition.

Schmeidler, G. R., ed. *Extrasensory Perception*
ALDINE-ATHERTON, INC.
529 SOUTH WABASH
CHICAGO, ILL. 60605
(Copyright 1969; clothbound, $6.95; paperback, $2.95)

This is a collection of six recent research papers and three articles about the ESP controversy. It may thus be regarded as an updating supplement to the Murphy and Dale survey. The experimental articles are concerned with various psychological factors, such as hypnosis, teacher-pupil attitudes, dreaming, and the difference in ESP scores between those who believe and those who disbelieve in the phenomenon. The editor has written a chatty introduction to the book and has followed each article with a brief personal response.

As required reading I suggest the critique by J. C. Crumbaugh (pp. 58–72), a psychologist who has worked off and on in parapsychology for 30 years without becoming fully convinced of the reality of ESP. My only substantial criticism of his excellent overview of the field is that I believe he is somewhat unsophisticated in his use of the concepts of "mechanism" and "scientific proof." For a discussion of mechanism I recommend H. Margenau, *The Nature of Physical Reality* (McGraw-Hill Book Co., Hightstown, N.J. 08520; copyright 1950; paperback, $3.95). For the study of scientific proof I suggest two books: T. S. Kuhn, *The Structure of Scientific Revolutions* (University of Chicago Press, 5750 Ellis Avenue, Chicago, Ill. 60637; copyright 1962; clothbound, $6.00, paperback, $1.50), and M. Polanyi, *Personal Knowledge* (University of Chicago Press; copyright 1958; $10.75). All three are difficult books.

Sinclair, U. *Mental Radio*
    CHARLES C THOMAS
    301 EAST LAWRENCE AVENUE
    SPRINGFIELD, ILL. 62703
    (Copyright 1930; 1962 edition, $8.50)

This is an original research report by a social reformer of the early twentieth century who took time off during a three-year period to study the

ESP picture-drawing ability of his wife. About two-thirds of her successful or partially successful drawings are presented, and the total number of attempts is stated. No statistical analysis is possible, but with results as dramatic as these, none is needed to allow one to decide that these drawings could not have resulted from chance coincidence or from "common memories" of the sender and receiver.

As in many great parapsychological experiments, all that is left as a counterexplanation is accidental or intentional deception by the experimenter. The question to be decided by every reader is: "Do you know this man well enough from his writing to judge whether he could have misled you under the circumstances described?" Here is a real-life mystery in which one can test his understanding of human nature. In this book there is a preface by Albert Einstein that indirectly reminds us that the game we are asked to play is not for amusement, but "for keeps."

As required reading for the student I suggest Upton Sinclair's own introduction (pp. xi–xiv, written for the 1962 edition some 30 years after the first publication), followed by pp. 111–128 (two chapters in which the author discusses the hypothesis of dishonesty and in which his wife tells how to develop one's own psychic ability). A more nearly complete discussion of the question of self-training will be found in the 1964 paper by Rhea White (see below).

The student who reads all of Sinclair's book will then profit by examining Rosalind Heywood's description of it in *Beyond the Reach of*

Sense (p. 140) and Gertrude Schmeidler's brief comment in her anthology *Extrasensory Perception* (p. 7) and can judge for himself whether these authors correctly reflect the scope and value of Sinclair's work.

In Appendix 1, in the course of examining "credibility in science," I have described Sinclair's work briefly and included a few of the target pictures and ESP responses from his book.

Smythies, J. R., ed. *Science and ESP*
ROUTLEDGE AND KEGAN PAUL, LTD.
68–74 CARTER LANE
LONDON E.C.4, ENGLAND

HUMANITIES PRESS, INC.
303 PARK AVENUE SOUTH
NEW YORK, N.Y. 10010
(Copyright 1967; $7.50)

This collection of scholarly essays relating the findings of parapsychology to other areas of knowledge has been included to provide a standard for the evaluation of the hundreds of popular books that have a somewhat similar intent. The essays of this volume are of mixed quality, and most of the book is too difficult for a beginner. By comparing chapters, the advanced student can study how difficult it is to separate sense and nonsense in a "pretheoretical" field of science. The numbers at the beginning of the following paragraphs refer to the chapters of the book.

1. A typically British, dialectical approach to the question, "Is ESP possible?"
2. How does a highly educated scholar re-

spond when he finds ESP inescapable? An answer is given by this 1952 Presidential Lecture to the Society for Psychical Research by a distinguished Oxford professor of Greek whose years of informal experimentation with telepathy convinced him of its reality while his "common sense" made him reject the possibility of precognition and psychokinesis. His case illustrates the ideological disarray widespread among the (parapsychological) party faithful.

3. A down-to-earth, easy-to-read discussion of the age-old mind-body problem in relation to ESP by H. H. Price, a classical philosopher of great distinction.

4. Brief comments on the changing attitudes of orthodoxy toward ESP.

5. These 80 pages reveal a proud and brilliant mind struggling with problems too big for our time—a mind bound, in the end, by its own culture. Because this chapter by Sir Cyril Burt is the most important part of the book, I shall discuss it at some length.

Psychologists know Sir Cyril Burt as Britain's leading authority on the measurement of mental ability. His pioneer studies on the method of "factor analysis" and on the similarity of identical twins are cornerstones supporting the now widely accepted idea that at least in West European populations the determination of human intelligence is 80 percent by heredity and 20 percent by environment.

Few psychologists are aware that Burt has long accepted and aggressively endorsed the evidence for ESP. He evidently believes that parapsychology is the future mainstream of psychology—that the tail will soon be wagging the dog.

Under the title "Psychology and Parapsychology" his essay deals with: the psychology of the skeptic; the metaphysical presuppositions of the materialist; idealism versus physicalism; mechanism, old and new; modern physics and the nature of science; the antecedent improbability of ESP; physical possibilities for the transmission of ESP; the implications of consciousness; and the possibility of postmortem survival of personality.

Burt's article is worthy of the *Encyclopaedia Britannica*. His vast and demonstrated scholarship provides a treasury of references. His endorsements and condemnations are colorful, verging on the simplistic. The layman who wants to achieve a sophistication concerning the philosophy of science that will exceed the understanding of most scientists has only to master the first 20 pages of Burt's essay.

He bludgeons modern behaviorists and their resistance to the possibility of ESP. They hardly deserve such an obliterative attack, but it is convenient for us to have it all in print to avoid the need for arguing with our less fortunate colleagues.

From a man born in 1883 and writing today, this is a truly remarkable autobiographical document.

6. Sir Alister Hardy, an Oxford zoologist, states his belief in the importance of ESP this

way: "The discovery that individuals are some-how in communication with one another by extra-sensory means is, if true, undoubtedly one of the most revolutionary discoveries ever made. It is a biological phenomenon, if true, almost as fundamental as that of gravity between material bodies." Hardy himself has accepted the reality of ESP for 20 years or more. In this essay he ranges from the possibility of consciousness in animals to the speculation that structural homology in evolution may involve a telepathic sharing of information.

7. A classical étude on the logical meaning of "precognition," by Philosophy Professor C. D. Broad of Cambridge University, born in 1887 and still a Titan among mortals. (Statistical neophytes please note: On p. 173 someone has substituted "contingency" and "contingent to" for "independence" and "independent of.")

8. A philosopher labors over the ideas of telepathy versus clairvoyance and physicalistic versus dualistic explanations thereof. Recommended reading for philosophers.

9. Professor Henry Margenau, the well-known Yale philosopher-physicist, (1) summarizes the attributes of any good theory, (2) reviews the more general laws of physics and their vulnerability as eternal verities, and (3) shows that the philosophic anomalies of modern physics are not helpful in trying to explain psychic phenomena. His book *The Nature of Physical Reality,* available in paperback (McGraw-Hill Book Co., 330 W. 42 Street, New York, N.Y. 10036; copyright

1950; $3.95), is a must for those who have a tendency to make theories.

10. A caricature of Burt's essay in the same volume. Especially worthwhile as a specimen of medieval scholasticism.

11. A brief statement about the interest of Freud and Freudians in parapsychology.

12. Carl Jung, perhaps even more than Sigmund Freud, perceived the depth of the question, "What are we?" Although we must reject his conceptions as scientifically incomprehensible, we may accept them as the intimations of genius concerning truth awaiting more systematic exploration.

13. Under the title "Anthropology and ESP" Francis Huxley of Oxford gives us a difficult and important discussion of primitive religious rituals and their possible relation to ESP.

Appendix: A nondescript collection of titles offered as "A Guide to the Evidence for ESP."

Soal, S. G., and F. Bateman. *Modern Experiments in Telepathy*
FABER & FABER, LTD.
3 QUEEN SQUARE
LONDON W.C.1N-3AU, ENGLAND
(1954; 30 shillings)

This English book fully reports what is surely one of the ten most important experimental studies in the history of parapsychology. The book gives firsthand contact with the card-guessing type of ESP research, which, for professional scientists, is the principal evidential underpinning of the phenomenon. Easily understood, but a thoroughly dull story, honestly told. The student will learn that research—even revolutionary research—is likely to require painstaking attention to unexciting details. The statistical evaluations, largely relegated to appendices, can be accepted on faith, for they have never been criticized. (Both authors are professional mathematicians.) The first six chapters, which are a historical review of the field, contain some errors of fact and unjustified interpretations. Throughout the work the authors preach a certain amount of methodological nonsense, but no more than is commonplace in science. The serious reader should consult a condensation and criticism of the book that appeared in the *Journal of Parapsychology,* XVIII (December 1954) , 245–258.

White, Rhea A. "A Comparison of Old and New Methods of Response to Targets in ESP Experiments," *Journal of the American Society for Psychical Research,* LVIII, No. 1 (January 1964) , 21–56.

Can a person train himself to receive pictures by ESP? Much has been written on this question, particularly in the early days of psychical research, before the card-guessing era.

This article by Rhea White is the best recent systematic review of the matter. From the outstanding experimenters and sensitives of the last

80 years she has assembled several dozen relevant quotations-at-length, organizing and discussing them according to the apparent "steps" in the picture-receiving procedure; namely, (1) relaxation of the body, (2) distraction of the conscious mind, (3) waiting in a state of tension, (4) receiving and recognizing the ESP image.

The importance of this paper is twofold. For the critics of ESP it will demonstrate that the field is not peopled solely by enthusiastic amateurs whose competence, if any, lies in other fields, but that there are truly sophisticated workers who are struggling intensely and intelligently with psychological factors that are real but seemingly just beyond our present methodological grasp.

For those within the field this paper should provide both hope for an ultimate research breakthrough on the problem of repeatability and guidance on the psychological essentials of the task immediately ahead.

This article is necessary reading for serious students of ESP, whether they wish to do research or merely to grasp the subtle nature of the phenomenon and to understand more fully why it is ignored by psychologists who must "publish or perish." The problem of this field in relation to science as a whole is stated by Miss White in this memorable sentence: "Even in the physical world, an unexplored wilderness cannot be mapped, let alone civilized, until someone grants it enough reality to set foot upon it" (p. 49).

This journal is available in the libraries of

about 50 colleges and universities in the United States, but that fact is of little help to most secondary-school instructors. If there is sufficient demand, the article will be separately reprinted by the A.S.P.R. Requests should be directed to:

Miss Rhea White
c/o The American Society for Psychical Research
5 West 73 Street
New York, N.Y. 10023

Whyte, L. L. *The Unconscious Before Freud*
TAVISTOCK PUBLICATIONS LTD.
11 NEW FETTER LANE
LONDON EC4P 4EE, U.K.

(Original publication Basic Books, Inc., 1960. First published in Great Britain by Tavistock Publications Ltd., 1962. Published by Tavistock as Social Science Paperback 19 in 1967. Tavistock paperback available in the United States from Barnes & Noble, Inc., 105 Fifth Avenue, New York, N.Y. 10003; $2.75.)

This book is a short explanation and history of the unconscious as an idea. For the hasty reader I recommend Chapters 1–4 and 8–9, skipping most of Chapters 5–7, which document the period before 1850.

This is an intellectually exciting book in its own right, but I am listing it here because it is the only one I know that provides the correct historical perspective for parapsychology. ESP and PK are unconscious phenomena, and as such are to be understood, not in terms of academic psychology, from which they were excluded, but in the total context of developing European thought from 1600 onward.

Just as T. S. Kuhn (see Index), by his theory of scientific revolutions, gives parapsychology legitimacy as an intruder upon the scientific community, so Whyte, by exposing the origins of the unconscious, makes parapsychology an unsurprising arrival on the philosophic scene. An interesting feature of this is that neither Kuhn nor Whyte says anything about ESP.

When I first came upon Whyte's book in 1962 I was inclined to suppose that his omission of psi phenomena was a tactically deliberate avoidance of controversy. Subsequently, in personal correspondence I discovered him to be curiously resistant to learning anything about ESP. I have concluded that Whyte, like Maxwell, Planck, and Einstein (to choose famous examples from physics), was so exhausted by his daring intellectual climb that he could not enjoy the view from his mountaintop.

Whyte is a lay essayist and lecturer to whom scientists listen with respect. I have heard him introduced as "the last Renaissance man." I prefer to hope that his intellectual breadth typifies the twenty-first century.

The message of his book is summed up in this sentence: "The term 'unconscious mental processes' is the enunciation of a program of research: to discover the true structure and function of mentality in terms of a single doctrine replacing the dualism which has broken down" (1960 ed., p. 56).

The unconscious is not the creation of Sigmund Freud, any more than ESP is that of J. B. Rhine. Whyte's book provides a broad look at the idea of the unconscious, in which Freud, shorn of theory and jargon, assumes his rightful place as a genius who, while Cartesian dualism was becoming increasingly intolerable, assembled some of the main girders for the future bridge between materialism and idealism. (The first five pages of the last chapter of Whyte's book summarize Freud's contribution to our world view.)

I am frequently asked, "What do you see as the future of parapsychology?" Having no time to write a book of speculation and expecting to be misunderstood if I speak briefly, I have kept silent. The happy thought occurs to me now that perhaps I might write a few sentences safely by stipulating that they are to be understood in the context of this book by Whyte.

The future task of psychology, as I see it, is to investigate the unconscious. Understanding will come in terms of the psychophysiology of the brain. Initially, psi phenomena will suggest constraints within which the solution must be found. At a later stage these phenomena will be crucial psychological tools. The first practical outcome of this research, whether early or later, may be a public realization that increasing the student's self-awareness is the only proper aim of education—insofar as "education" is not training.

OMITTED BOOKS*

From my list I have omitted a number of otherwise worthwhile books now in print that I believe are too difficult, specialized, or speculative, or in some cases misleadingly uncritical in accepting supposed empirical facts.

With reluctance I omit Collier Books' paperback translation of René Warcollier's *Mind to Mind* (Crowell Collier and Macmillan, 866 Third Avenue, New York, N.Y. 10022, $.95). This work abstracts Warcollier's 1910–35 picture-drawing experiments and primitive psychological theorizing. In retrospect, his arduous labors appear as a methodological blind alley that deserves exploration by every professional parapsychologist but that may mislead or discourage the beginner.

Another omitted work is C. D. Broad's *Lectures on Psychical Research,* which is important to professional parapsychologists as an introduc-

---

* In this section I am referring to omitted books that might have some appeal to the critical and sophisticated mind. These are only a small part of the books in print in the area known loosely as "the occult arts and sciences." In Appendix 2 I have added a survey of the sale of occult books so that the reader may see how parapsychology relates (or fails to relate) to the interests of the common man.

tion to the early journal literature and for the study of this classical philosopher's evaluation thereof (Routledge and Kegan Paul, 68–74 Carter Lane, London, Eng., 1962; Humanities Press, 303 Park Avenue South, New York, N.Y. 10010; $10.00). This book as a whole differs from Murphy and Dale's *Challenge of Psychical Research* in two ways: (1) Although twice as long, only 23 percent of its pages are given to experimental ESP and none to PK. (2) Its author does not stay close to the original literature but allows himself freedom to interpret and speculate.

There are several biographical works that belong in any professional library of parapsychology but that will have only limited value for the layman. Important among these is Alan Gauld's *The Founders of Psychical Research* (Routledge and Kegan Paul, London, 1968; handled in the U.S. by Schocken Books, Inc., 67 Park Avenue, New York, N.Y. 10016; $10.00) .

I have also passed over all books, however scholarly and courageous, that attempt to join parapsychology and mysticism. A reasoned connection between these two subjects can be made at this time only by erecting a theoretical structure so far beyond empirical validation as to violate the canons of scientific method. I do not doubt that there is a connection that will some day be discovered. I am convinced that mystical experience, in the broad sense of that term, is of the highest significance in determining the motivation of individuals and the fate of a society.

But I see no gain in mixing science with dogma, whether from the West or the East. The student of science must learn a patient willingness to say, "I do not know, and I shall probably never know; although perhaps my children will."

IV SYLLABUS

HOW DISCOVERIES ARE MADE IN SCIENCE

This section, on the nature of science, may be expanded or compressed in the classroom depending upon how well the topic has been previously covered. One of the best available explanations of how science "works" is found in *The Structure of Scientific Revolutions* (University of Chicago Press, 5750 Ellis Avenue, Chicago, Ill. 60637, 1962; cloth bound, $6.00, paperback, $1.50), by Professor T. S. Kuhn of Princeton University. However, this is a difficult book to read. A short, easy condensation of it has been printed in the *Journal of the American Society for Psychical Research,* LXII (1968), 321–327. Single copies of this condensation may be obtained by sending a postcard to the author of this curriculum guide.

The Two Basic Requirements of Scientific Method

Science requires both theory and observation. Pure theory occurs only in mathematics. Mathematics by itself is merely a tool—or an art form, if one is inclined to view it that way. Pure observation occurs in everyday living. When one takes time to classify and organize observations, one has the beginnings of science or pre-science.

The Nature of Theory

Theory is the statement of a recognized pattern or relationship in the world around us. In other words, a theory is a generalization based on observation. Theory does not "explain" in an absolute sense why an event occurs. Theory merely predicts that a certain event will occur (observation can be made) if certain conditions have been met (i.e., other observations have been made).

Theories are sometimes classified as "big" or "little" depending upon their scope. Little theories deal only with subtopics of a field of science. Big theories cover areas large enough to have philosophic interest in their own right.

Normal Science versus Scientific Revolutions

When one major theory contradicts another, a scientific revolution occurs. "Normal science" is the peaceful situation in which most scientists agree on the over-all theories in a field. Contradictory little theories lead to scientific quarrels but not to "wars." Most scientists spend their time building little theories and try to avoid anxiety-generating controversy about the big theories they were taught in their youth.

In a new field there may be many little theories, but until the first widely encompassing theory is generally accepted, it is debatable whether a "field of science" can be said to exist. This is where ESP stands today. It is a fact without an over-all theory. One suspects that it will someday cause a revolution in both psychology and physics.

The whole problem of controversy, revolution, and credibility in science is one of great human interest. In Appendix 1, in a slightly autobiographical vein, I have tried to capture some of the excitement of a scientist's intellectual struggle with his colleagues.

The Nature of Observation

Observations may be classified as "naturalistic" or "controlled." Some writers use the longer terms "naturalistic observations" and "controlled experimentation."

In naturalistic observation, the scientist tries to be present with his tools when interesting things are happening over which he has no control. In experimentation, he causes events to occur, preferably while measuring some conditions and holding constant others that might be important.

The Relation of Theory to Observation

A new field of science usually begins with the uncontrolled observation of spontaneous events. These may first be organized into a useful art or technology (as metallurgy preceded chemistry). Eventually the known facts suggest hypotheses (tentative theories). These theories then allow predictions that can be tested by controlled experimentation. The data of the experiments may confirm the theory or may suggest its modification. In this way, theory and experiment develop hand in hand. For scientific purposes one is incomplete without the other.

SPONTANEOUS PSI PHENOMENA

In the source documents (but not the textbooks) of history there are many reported instances in which a person gained presumably inaccessible knowledge or feeling about a distant or future event. In these cases the percipient usually had some psychological connection with the event, as in the death of a loved one. Sometime in their lives many or most people living today have at least one recognizable ESP occurrence. A few people have such occurrences rather frequently.

Since these events contradict our everyday experience with space-time happenings, they create conflict or dissonance in our perception of the universe. Systematic thinkers are especially prone to "anomaly anxiety." Thus there exists the ironic situation in which most scientists reject ESP because "It does not fit," while the uneducated man cheerfully accepts this part of reality that he or his friends have observed.

There is a classical escape from this dilemma, namely, repeatable laboratory experimentation. There is no reason why all natural phenomena should be repeatable at will, and psychic phenomena generally are not. Fortunately, some minor kinds of ESP *can* (sometimes) be produced by trying in the laboratory, although we do not know all of the conditions necessary. At the risk of offending more formally inclined scientists by my anthropomorphism, I suggest that we should be grateful to nature for having given us at least this much of a toehold on experimentation, by which we may reasonably hope someday to unravel this puzzle and achieve scientific understanding. (One might compare this with the toehold given us on nuclear energy by the occurrence of a trace of the isotope U-235 in natural uranium. Without that trace the discovery of fission might have been delayed a long time.)

Perhaps further mention should be made of those few people who experience much ESP. Many of them find that it creates a personal problem. Such people may have unnecessary fears about their sanity. Often they encounter ridicule. Some turn to religion for comfort; others manage to suppress their ESP ability; most learn to keep their thoughts to themselves. From the telephone calls I receive I would estimate that, to within a factor of ten, the fraction of the American population who are bothered by their outstanding ESP ability is one in a thousand. One urgent, humanitarian reason for the universal study of ESP in our schools is to give these specially gifted people a happier life and perhaps some day a chance to use their abilities creatively.

The classroom discussion of spontaneous ESP

will develop of its own accord around cases observed by the students, their families, and friends. Counterexplanations, including mere chance coincidence, should be considered. Is there anything left that needs an explanation? How could one go about investigating such cases? The difficulty of eliminating ordinary explanations from unplanned observation points to the importance of controlled experimentation.

EXPERIMENTAL PARAPSYCHOLOGY

The instructor may wish to confine discussion to several of the better-known ways of demonstrating psi phenomena. To an imaginative person it will be evident that there are endless experimental possibilities. Most of these, however, will present psychological, procedural, instrumental, or analytical difficulties, which must be discovered and overcome. Thus the presentation suggested herein for the classroom has been largely restricted to two kinds of ESP (picture drawing and card guessing) and to one kind of PK (placement psychokinesis).

Picture Drawing

Trying to draw a hidden picture by ESP can be fun. This is called a "free-response" method of experimenting, because the subject matter of the target is unknown. The guessing of a playing card, on the other hand, is called an "alternative-choice" test, because the perceiving subject is asked merely to make a selection among given possibilities.

Free-response targets allow a greater range for the operation of ESP and sometimes yield dramatic results. Moreover, the freedom of the task helps in maintaining the atmosphere of relaxation that is believed conducive to the appearance of ESP. On the other hand, ESP pictures are more difficult to evaluate than card guesses.

Sometimes the ESP pictures are so strikingly correct in detail that they can be labeled "right" or "partly right" to the satisfaction of most independent judges. The long series of pictures in the Upton Sinclair book are among the best examples of this sort of thing.

However, when one desires a rigorously correct probability figure, the usual method of evaluation is to identify the target pictures and response drawings by code numbers only and to ask one or more judges to try to match them— for form, content, or otherwise.

As in any ESP research, aside from the mechanical arrangements, the main responsibility of the experimenter is to try to establish the unknown psychological conditions for success. I believe that the following suggestions will convey a correct impression of what are generally regarded as the "necessary but not sufficient conditions" for ESP to appear.

The percipient should be motivated to know the specific target. This may be through the personal meaningfulness of the target, or because of a wish to please the experimenter, or as an expression of desire for achievement, or because of any sufficiently strong factor.

The target should be psychologically specific, as by having a definite location in time and space and by having the percipient fully aware of, if not actually attentive to, the facts or conditions that isolate that target from all other possible targets.

The subject must be in the proper mood. For an average person this is believed to mean quiet relaxation, an absence of anxiety, a blank mind or perhaps the state of thinking about a trivial task. Although spectacular psychics are known to use exhausting concentration, if you are a beginner, trying "too hard" may prevent success. The best available information on the self-development of ESP ability is given in the paper by Rhea White described in the bibliography.

The mechanical procedures necessary to eliminate the possibilities of error and fraud must be made as unobtrusive as possible. Preferably, the entire procedure should appear as a game to the percipient.

The procedure for a picture-drawing experiment is given in Appendix 3.

Card Guessing

Card-guessing methods of experimentation dominated the literature of ESP after J. B. Rhine emphasized them in his first book in 1934 (reviewed in the bibliography). Today they are little used in their original forms, but the guessing of other kinds of independent targets with a fixed, known probability of success is of continuing importance.

Card guessing is the simplest ESP experiment to perform in the classroom and not at all difficult to evaluate statistically. The chief objection to cards is that most participants, after the first few decks, find them uninteresting. Spontaneity and motivation are believed essential for eliciting ESP. Some teachers, by ingenuity and vivacity, overcome this limitation of cards in a short experiment. In any case, it is certainly true that there are few participants who can avoid boredom and continue to produce ESP by means of cards over a lengthy test period.

A description of a card-guessing experiment and its method of analysis are given in Appendix 4.

Psychokinesis

PK experiments have generally been of two types—"die-face" and "placement." Die-face experiments typically consist of wishing for particular die faces to come uppermost when one to six gaming dice are thrown simultaneously from a rough-lined cup against a felt-covered backboard into a felt-lined tray (or by a machine). Placement experiments are usually performed by releasing dice or unmarked cubes above a table while wishing them to come to rest on one side or the other of the tabletop.

I recommend placement experiments for school use because they provide opportunities for dramatic psychokinetic motion (whether or not such motion is actually identifiable) and minimize the recording error problem, while at the same time they avoid a "gambling aura," to which the uninformed might take exception. The placement method is relatively new, lends itself to numerous modifications, and is a hopeful tool for developing a person's PK ability.

The building of placement apparatus should be an interesting task for a mechanically-minded student. General instructions for this are given in Appendix 5.

Outline instructions for a placement experiment are provided in Appendix 6. The actual performance of PK experiments may need to be carried out singly or in small groups, after school hours, unless it is found that the wishing of an entire class can be "orchestrated" by the teacher—a challenging prospect indeed.

ESP AND CREDIBILITY IN SCIENCE*

In discussing extrasensory perception before psychology students, it is not uncommon to stress the credulity of the public. Perhaps, instead, we ought to examine the credibility of scientists—including those on both sides of the controversy.

In ESP research whom shall we trust? One can rather easily imagine experimental precautions to keep participating subjects from cheating. But how do we know whether the experimenter is deliberately deceiving us? And in a world where people believe all kinds of nonsense, how can we be sure that the experimenter is not deceiving himself?

Let us suppose that 10 experimenters independently get the same result. Can we accept it? Ten is not a large number. There are about 150,000 names in *American Men of Science*. We may reasonably assume that at least 10,000 of these hold beliefs about the nature of reality that the majority of scientists would regard as wholly without foundation. Thus, on a subject like ESP, where there are no recognized authorities, why should we accept the word of 10 experimenters—

* An invited lecture to the introductory psychology classes at Carnegie-Mellon University, December 18 and 19, 1967. Copyright 1969 by the American Psychological Association, Inc.; reprinted from *The American Psychologist,* XXIV 531–538.

or, for that matter, a thousand? Are we not, all of us, creatures of our culture? Is there any way we can be sure that a scientist in any field is as rational as he pretends to be?

Questions concerning the credibility of scientists are rarely asked in our classrooms. I have wondered why. Perhaps it makes us uncomfortable to consider the possibility of incompetence, dishonesty, or mental illness among professional people. Whatever the reason, this is forbidden territory for study.

Once in a long while these embarrassing ideas do come to the surface. Someone, a little bolder or a little more eccentric than the rest of us, may write an article that slips by the editorial censor. When that happens we have a chance to learn what people really think.

When I accepted this invitation to talk to you I was told I could give you an advance reading assignment. I asked that you read an eight-page article on ESP by G. R. Price (1955) that appeared in *Science* together with several letters to the editor (Soal, Rhine, Meehl and Scriven, Bridgman, Price, Rhine—1956) written in reply to Price. These papers are currently available as part of the Bobbs-Merrill reprint series that is widely used for teaching psychology, and they have thus acquired a quasi-official status as source documents to which the very young may be exposed.

I also suggested that you read an analysis of Price's article (McConnell, 1955) that appeared in the *Journal of Parapsychology* and that was not included in the Bobbs-Merrill series. I hope that most of you have had a chance to study these references, which I shall now discuss briefly.

Price, a chemist by profession, presented a well-supported argument showing that existing experimental evidence constitutes conclusive proof of ESP if one accepts the good faith and sanity of the experimenters. But he went on to say that all of the otherwise convincing evidence for ESP can be easily explained away if one assumes that experimenters, working in collaboration with their witnesses, have intentionally faked their results.

Perhaps the most interesting thing about this unsubstantiated suggestion of fraud is that it was published on the first page of the most influential scientific journal in the United States. I will not say whether Price intended what he wrote as a joke. That is a riddle that I leave to you to answer. The important question is not whether Price took himself seriously, but whether you and I ought to do so.

I believe, as apparently does Price, that all kinds of fraud, even by highly placed scientists, are possible and that it is conceivable that there might be collaboration between two scientists in perpetuating a scientific hoax. Nevertheless I think that those who accept Price's argument fail to understand two important things about science as a social enterprise.

First, they fail to realize that the way to tell whether a number of scientists are collaborating in a hoax is to consider the intricate web of public and private motivation, belief, and retribution that determines the behavior of professional people in our culture. Price suggested that scientists, university teachers, medical doctors, and intellectually prominent persons who have assisted in the investigation of ESP may have engaged in conscious collusive fraud. Price answered the question of how one might get such people to become willing accomplices by saying, "In recruiting, I would appeal not to desire for fame or material gain but to the noblest motives, arguing that much good to humanity could result from a small deception designed to strengthen religious belief." An experienced lawyer or even a politician would laugh at this explanation of a supposed conspiracy among well-educated and fully engaged members of our society, but evidently quite a few scientists find it plausible.

Second, those scientists who take Price seriously do not understand scientific method. Price suggested that the way to establish the scientific truth of ESP is to carry out a fraudproof experiment. In his words, "What is needed is one completely convincing experiment." He described in specific detail how this might be done by using prominent scientists and stage magicians as witnesses, backed up by motion pictures of the entire proceedings, plus photomicrographs of welded seals, and so on. This is nonsense, because it assumes that scientific proof is of the same nature as legal proof. On the contrary, the acceptance of a scientific principle does not, and never can, depend upon the honesty of individual scientists.

I wish I had time to pursue with you the subtle psychological question of the nature of scientific proof and of how the method of science deals with individual experimenter error as well as mass irrationality. Those of you who are especially interested may wish to read a book by T. S. Kuhn (1962) titled *The Structure of Scientific Revolutions*.* Here today I can only say that in my opinion, wittily or unwittingly, Price's article is a hoax about hoaxes and about the nature of science.

If you were to ask, "What does it signify that Price successfully placed his article in our most important journal of science?" I would answer as follows: There is a façade of respectability and belief that covers all of the activities of society and makes it possible for men to work together and for society to exist. Most people—including those who are well educated—are unaware of this false front and lose their equilibrium when they are forced by circumstances to penetrate behind it. On the other hand, those of you who are intellectually alienated from our culture understand quite well that this pretense exists. I hope that some day you will also understand why it is necessary and that it is not the contrivance of a group of evil men but reflects what existential philosophers refer to as "the human condition."

---

* For a condensation of this book see McConnell (1968b).

This curtain of propriety and convention exists in science also, where it allows us to believe that all is well with our knowledge system. ESP or any other revolutionary discovery may seem to threaten science. From time to time, when such a challenge is offered, the stagehands nervously fumble, the curtain slips, and we see a little of the normally concealed machinery. We get a glimpse of underlying reality, a glimpse of the ignorance and fear that govern the inner affairs of the mind of man. Such was the case when *Science* published Price's critique of ESP. That is why his article is important.

Evidence and Belief

Then, what about ESP? If laboratory scientists lack sophistication about human nature and even about the methodology of science, how do we decide for ourselves whether ESP is real or imaginary, true or false?

Before we try to answer so difficult a question, let us go back to the beginning. I shall give you an operational definition of ESP that you may find a bit confusing. Then I shall describe a test for ESP that I hope will make the matter clear to you.

The definition goes this way: "Extrasensory perception is a response to an unknown event not presented to any known sense." I shall not try to explain it. Instead, let me describe the test.

I have brought with me a deck of ESP cards. These cards have five different kinds of symbols printed on them: a circle, a square, a plus, a star, and wavy lines. Altogether there are 25 cards, 5 of each kind.

Suppose I shuffle these cards, hide them, and ask you to guess them. By the theory of chance probability, the number you would most often get right is 5. Sometimes you would get 4 or 6 or 7. Only once in a long while would you get 15 right out of 25. In fact, if you got more than 10 right very often, you would begin to suspect that it was not just good luck. It might even be ESP.

Of course, you could not be sure. It might be luck—or it might be something else. If you look closely at the backs of these cards, sometimes you can see the symbol showing through. Perhaps in this way you recognized some of the cards when I shuffled them. Or again, every time I asked whether you were ready for your next guess, perhaps I gave you a hint without knowing it. Perhaps, unconsciously, I raised the tone of my voice just a little when I came to each star—because I think of stars as being "higher" than the other symbols, or for some other trivial reason.

You can see that there are many subtle ways for information to leak through by sight or by sound. No serious scientist would try to conduct an ESP experiment in this fashion. My only purpose in showing you these cards is to let you know how some of the early tests for ESP were done at Duke University 35 years ago. I regard these cards as a museum piece, although they are a lot of fun and can be used in preliminary testing.

The experiments that are carried out today

are often so complex that one cannot evaluate them without advanced training in statistics, physics, and psychology. For this reason, and because the field is too large to describe in one lecture, I have prepared a list of reading materials. Some of these are intended to show the scope of the subject (Heywood, 1964; Langdon-Davies, 1961; McConnell, 1966; Murphy and Dale, 1961) ; others are experimental reports (Anderson and McConnell, 1961; McConnell and Forwald, 1967a, 1967b, 1968; McConnell, Snowdon, and Powell, 1955; Sinclair, 1962; Soal and Bateman, 1954) .

You will notice that I have listed only my own journal articles. For this I offer my apology along with the following explanation. In any frontier field of science there are experimental hazards. If someone questions the soundness of what I recommend to you as evidence, I can probably do a better job of explaining if I have chosen research with which I am most familiar. I also want to convey the idea that there has been a large amount of work done in this field. If you study my papers and cannot find anything wrong with them, you ought to remember that there have been perhaps a hundred other investigators who have found substantial evidence for ESP under controlled experimental conditions.

ESP is a controversial idea in psychology. Nevertheless the psychologists whom I know personally agree with me on many things. I am sure we agree on what constitutes good-quality experimental laboratory research. We also agree that there is a sizable body of high-grade evidence for ESP in the literature.

In 1947 I visited Duke University in North Carolina, where a man by the name of Rhine was doing experiments on ESP. I wanted to get acquainted with Rhine and with the people who were working under him. Even more important, I wanted to talk to those faculty members who rejected Rhine's work. I rented a dormitory room, and during four weeks I interviewed everyone I could, beginning with the president of the university and working down to assistant professors in various departments. I shall not have time to describe that adventure, but I will tell you what I was told by one professor of psychology in a private interview.

He said that he was familiar with the experimental literature of ESP and that, in his opinion, if it were anything else *but* ESP, one-tenth of the published evidence would already have established the phenomenon. He also explained that he would not accept ESP himself because, as he put it, he found "a world without ESP a more comfortable place in which to live."

That trip to Duke University was part of a larger investigation that made me decide to leave engineering electronics, in which I had acquired some experience, and to devote my life to the investigation of ESP and related effects.

That was 20 years ago. What has happened in this field since then? Among other things, there has been time to publish 20 more volumes of the *Journal of Parapsychology*. That comes to about

4,000 pages of research. There have been several thousand additional pages in the *Journal of the American Society for Psychical Research* and in the English and Continental journals. You might think that the argument would be settled by now.

Only recently a brilliant young psychologist, who is here on your campus, gave a lecture on ESP in which he said, "I tend to believe the evidence is as good as it is for many of our other psychological phenomena." He also said, "Psychologists will not be interested in ESP until there is a repeatable experiment."

The manner in which my psychologist friends and I disagree is that I believe that the available evidence for ESP is sufficient to establish its reality beyond all reasonable doubt; my psychologist friends think that the evidence is not yet conclusive. I do not regard this difference of opinion as very important. I am happy to allow anyone the privilege of doubt.

How else does the position of professional psychologists whom I know differ from my own? Perhaps the main difference—the really important difference—lies in our interpretation of the history and methodology of science—in what today we call the philosophy of science.

For one thing, my friends seem to believe that the only good evidence for ESP must come from controlled experimentation in a laboratory. My own belief is that all available evidence must be weighed, taking into account its source and the conditions under which it was gathered.

Perhaps it will clarify the problem if I say that there are only two important kinds of scientific evidence in this world: our own evidence and someone else's. Since most of us are not in a position to gather evidence of ESP, my remarks apply especially to other people's evidence.

The first thing to remember is that, no matter how reputable the scientific journal, someone else's evidence is always suspect. And if the matter is important, we ought to be *aggressively* skeptical about it.

Whether we are listening to a tale of a ghost in a haunted house or reading the tightly edited *Journal of Experimental Psychology*, we have to concern ourselves with two questions: what is the content of the report and what are the competence and motivation of the observer?

What I am suggesting is that our attitude toward *all* supposedly scientific reports must be that of the psychologist in receiving an introspective account from a human subject in a laboratory experiment—for it must be remembered that, as far as the reader is concerned, a journal article by a distant scientist is in some ways even less dependable than what psychologists, often condescendingly, refer to as a "verbal report."

From a study of the history of science I have come to two conclusions in this connection: (a) the evidence presented in scientific journals by professional scientists for all kinds of ordinary phenomena is not as good as commonly supposed, and (b) on a controversial subject where the professionals do not agree, the evidence of the layman may have considerable scientific value.

As corollaries, I suggest that the textbooks of science are often wrong and that contrary popular opinion is sometimes right. Let us examine these ideas.

Storehouses of Knowledge?

Textbooks are the storehouses of man's knowledge. They are presumed to contain all of the things we know to be true. If you are becoming a scientist, you will spend at least 18 years studying from books. It would be not entirely unfair to call most of this training a "brainwashing" process. Nearly everything you learn as factual reality must be accepted upon the word of some recognized authority and not upon your own firsthand experience. It should be a matter of concern to you whether you have been told the truth for those 18 years. Just how bad are the textbooks we use? Let me take an example from the field of geology.

Did you know that until the year 1800 the highest scientific authorities thought that there was no such thing as a meteorite? After all, there are no stones in the sky; so stones cannot fall out of the sky. Only a superstitious person would believe in meteorites.

Many of you are familiar with the work of Lavoisier. He was the founder of modern chemistry. He discovered that burning is the combining of oxygen with other things, and he helped to show that the formula for water is H_2O. He was one of the great scientists of all time.

In 1772 Lavoisier signed a report to the

French Academy of Science in which he said he had examined a stone that was believed to have fallen from the sky in a great blaze of light. Lavoisier said in his report that this was just an ordinary stone that had been struck by lightning and had melted partly into glass while lying on the ground.

Eventually, of course, the leaders of science decided that meteorites do come from outer space, and they revised the textbooks accordingly. But in doing so they forgot to mention that there had ever been any argument about the matter. So here we are, living in the space age, without realizing how hard it is to discover the truth about even a simple thing like meteorites, which can be seen as meteors in the sky on any clear night, and which have been found upon the surface of the earth since the dawn of history.

Even worse, as students we have no way of estimating how many arguments are still going on in science and how many mistakes—truly serious mistakes—there are in the textbooks from which we study. It is my guess that we can safely believe nearly all of what is said in the physics and chemistry books. But we ought to believe only half of the ideas in the biological sciences—although I am not sure which half. And we should accept as final very little in the social sciences, which try to explain why groups of people behave as they do.

Our subject today is extrasensory perception, which belongs in psychology, one of the biological sciences. ESP is something about which the "authorities" are in error. Most psychology textbooks omit the subject entirely as unworthy of serious attention. But these books are mistaken, because ESP is a real psychological phenomenon.

Of course, I am only giving you my individual opinion about ESP. I do not want you to base your belief upon what I tell you. When you have studied advanced psychology and statistics, and when you come to realize that your professors cannot be expected to teach you everything you wish to know, then I hope you will go to the scientific journals and study the experiments that have been done and decide for yourself.

Mental Radio

I have already discussed the credibility of experts and the errors we find in science textbooks. I would like to turn next to the other half of my thesis, namely, that evidence from a layman may sometimes have scientific value.

Most of you are familiar with the name of Upton Sinclair, who was a socialist reformer and a writer active in the first half of the twentieth century. He died in 1968 at the age of ninety. In his time he wrote nearly 90 books. One of the best known of these, published in 1906, was called *The Jungle*. It told about the cruel and unsanitary conditions in the processing of beef in the Chicago stockyards. As a result of that book laws were passed, and today the situation is much improved. In a very real sense, all of us are indebted to this man.

Sinclair discovered that his wife had an unusual amount of what was then known as "psychic ability." (That was before the beginning of the ESP controversy.) After three years of serious experimentation he wrote a book about it: *Mental Radio* (1962; orig. pub., 1930) .

In his experiments Sinclair, or someone else, would draw a secret picture and ask Mrs. Sinclair to draw another picture to match it. Some of the pairs of pictures are presented in the following examples.* The one on the left is always the original picture, and the one on the right is what Mrs. Sinclair got by ESP.

Sometimes the pictures were made as far apart as 40 miles. At other times the target picture was held by Mrs. Sinclair in her hand—without looking, of course—while she concentrated before drawing her matching picture. The degree of success did not seem to depend upon distance.

Let us examine some of the pictures. In Example 1 we see an almost perfect ESP response.

Example 1

* Illustrations from *Mental Radio,* by Upton Sinclair, are reproduced by permission of the publisher, Charles C Thomas, Springfield, Illinois.

It is a knight's helmet. Notice that for every important line in the left-hand picture there is a corresponding line on the right.

Compare that with Example 2. Here the response on the right is not quite the same as the target on the left, but the idea is the same.

Example 2

The next one is Example 3. Sinclair drew a football as a target. Mrs. Sinclair made the drawing on the right, but she thought it was "a baby calf with a belly band." Why did her ESP

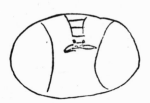 

Example 3

make this mistake? We cannot be sure, but we think it had something to do with the fact that in her childhood she had known a queer old man who raised calves as parlor pets and dressed them in embroidered bellybands.

Example 4 is another instance of the right shape with a wrong interpretation. Upton Sinclair drew a volcano, and Mrs. Sinclair drew what

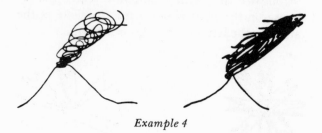

Example 4

she called a black beetle. The beetle is upside down. If you turn the example over, you can more easily recognize its antennae and legs.

In Example 5 Sinclair drew a fishhook, which turned into two flowers.

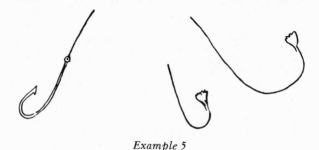

Example 5

Example 6 shows a fragmentary response. Sinclair drew a balloon. The response on the right is what his wife received by "mental radio." She was not sure what it was, so she wrote beside the

Example 6

picture: "Shines in sunlight, must be metal, a scythe hanging among vines or strings."

Example 7 on the left is a swastika. Mrs. Sinclair drew the response on the right. She did not know what it meant, but she wrote beside it: "These things somehow belong together, but

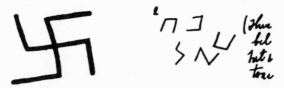

Example 7

won't get together." You can see some of her words, which were accidentally included when the printer made the book. Here is the beginning of "These" and "belong" and "but won't" and "together."

Example 8 is a pair of drawings in which a stick man became a skull and crossbones.

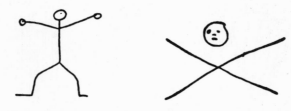

Example 8

Notice that in Example 9 Mrs. Sinclair left out some of the stars and added a moon instead.

Example 9

In Example 10 Sinclair drew an umbrella. His wife responded with this curious picture, which she described in writing beside it as follows: "I

Example 10

feel that it is a snake crawling out of something—vivid feeling of snake, but it looks like a cat's tail." I might mention that she had a special fear of snakes, having grown up on a plantation in a Mississippi swamp.

The last example is the American flag and a response to it that could hardly be called a chance coincidence (Example 11).

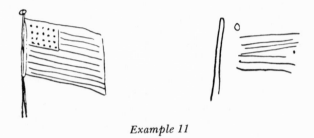

Example 11

You have seen a selection of 11 pictures out of a total of 290 trials made by Mrs. Sinclair. Perhaps 4 of the 11 would be called direct target hits. The rest are partial hits. Out of the 290 tries, 23 percent were rated by Upton Sinclair as hits, 53 percent were partial hits, and 24 percent were failures.

Of course, before you can be sure that these pictures were made by ESP, many questions must be answered. Because Upton Sinclair and his wife were laymen, you will have to pay particular attention to their competence and motivation. On the other hand, one important feature of Sinclair's book is that you do not have to be a scientist to understand it. Even though you may not have studied statistics and psychology, you can read the book yourself and make up your mind as to its value on the basis of common sense. When you do, I think you will arrive at the same conclusion that many scientists have reached by entirely different kinds of experiments. I think you will decide that extrasensory perception is a reality regardless of the skepticism of the psychological profession.

A Matter of Interest

I have been told by my friends that psychologists will not be interested in ESP until someone discovers a repeatable experiment. Upton Sinclair repeated his experiments over a period of three years. In London a mathematician by the name of Soal (Soal and Bateman, 1954) repeated certain card-guessing experiments again and again over a period of six years using two subjects and many different witnesses. What do psychologists mean by a repeatable experiment?

Evidently they mean an experiment that is "repeatable by prescription." They want a standard experimental procedure that can be described on paper by which any qualified person —or at least some qualified persons—can guarantee to produce ESP upon demand. I must confess that we have not yet reached that stage in ESP research. And, until we do, I can sympathize with my skeptical friends. I can see why they, as busy individuals with other interests, are unwilling to reach a firm position about the reality of ESP.

What I cannot understand is why they say, "Psychologists will not be *interested* in ESP until there is a repeatable experiment."

It is a statement of fact that psychologists are *not* interested in ESP. Recently I had occasion to examine a number of psychology textbooks. Only one of them mentioned ESP—a book by Hilgard and Atkinson (1967). After reading the four pages that these authors devote to ESP I have only two minor critical observations to offer.

The first is that the authors have given too much space to finding fault with unimportant papers. They go back 25 years to a journal article and accuse the author, an ESP experimenter, of overanalyzing his data. I am sure that comparable examples of weak statistical method could be found in any one of the quantitative journals of the American Psychological Association—and we would not need to go back a generation in time to do it.

My second comment is that Hilgard and Atkinson may have tended to damage their own scholarly reputations by recommending as a "scholarly review" a book by C. E. M. Hansel (1966) titled *ESP: A Scientific Evaluation*. This book has been reviewed by S. S. Stevens of Harvard, who regards ESP as a Rabelaisian joke and who gave Hansel his unqualified approval. If you like amusing book reviews, I suggest that you read Stevens (1967). I regret that I do not have time here today to document for you the basis of my unfavorable opinion of Hansel's book.*

I have wandered over many facets of ESP. I shall now summarize what I think are the most important ideas. Since the scientific study of ESP was begun by the London Society for Psychical Research in 1882, there have been hundreds and perhaps thousands of experiments done with a care typical of the journals of the American Psychological Association. Many psychologists of high repute admit that the evidence is as good as that for other phenomena that are accepted by their profession.

Surprising though it may seem, most of this research on ESP has been done by people who were not psychologists. From this fact and from the usual psychology textbook treatment of the subject, as well as from private discussion, we know that psychologists are *not* interested in ESP. This raises a question—a very mysterious question that I invite you to try to answer: Why are psychologists not interested in ESP?†

* This has been done elsewhere (McConnell, 1968a). Moreover, since the original publication of the appendix you are now reading, the position of parapsychology vis-à-vis academic psychology has changed. As of 1971 there are at least eight textbooks of general psychology giving favorable attention to ESP. The treatment of ESP in the 1971 edition of the Hilgard-Atkinson text has been strengthened. A statement from their 1967 edition (p. 243) questioning the possible social importance of ESP has disappeared, and their recommendation of Hansel's book has been shorn of any value judgment.

† Those who wish to answer this question might start their odyssey by visiting Clark et al. (1967) and Linder (1967).

REFERENCES

Anderson, M. L., and R. A. McConnell. "Fantasy Testing for ESP in a Fourth- and Fifth-Grade Class," *Journal of Psychology,* LII (1961) , 491–503.

Clark, K. E., *et al.* "The Scientific and Professional Aims of Psychology," *American Psychologist,* XXII (1967) , 49–76.

Hansel, C. E. M. *ESP: A Scientific Evaluation.* New York: Scribner's, 1966.

Heywood, R. *ESP: A Personal Memoir.* New York: Dutton, 1964.

Hilgard, E. R., and R. C. Atkinson. *Introduction to Psychology.* New York: Harcourt Brace Jovanovich, 1967.

Kuhn, T. S. *The Structure of Scientific Revolutions* (Vol. II, No. 2, of the *International Encyclopedia of Unified Science*) . Chicago: University of Chicago Press, 1962.

Langdon-Davies, J. *On the Nature of Man.* New York: New American Library Corporation, 1961.

Linder, R. "Light One Candle," *American Psychologist,* XXII (1967) , 804–805.

McConnell, R. A. "Price in *Science,*" *Journal of Parapsychology,* XIX (1955) , 258–261.

———. "ESP Research at Three Levels of Method," *Journal of Parapsychology,* XXX (1966) , 195–207.

———. "The ESP Scholar," *Contemporary Psychology,* XIII (1968) , 41 (a) .

———. "The Structure of Scientific Revolutions: An Epitome," *Journal of the American Society for Psychical Research,* LXII (1968) , 321–327 (b) .

McConnell, R. A. and H. Forwald. "Psychokinetic Placement: I. A Re-examination of the Forwald-Durham Experiment," *Journal of Parapsychology,* XXXI (1967) , 51–69 (a) .

———. "Psychokinetic Placement: II. A Factorial Study

of Successful and Unsuccessful Series," *Journal of Parapsychology*, XXXI (1967), 198–213 (b).

———. "Psychokinetic Placement: III. Cube-releasing Devices," *Journal of Parapsychology*, XXXII (1968), 9–38.

McConnell, R. A., R. J. Snowdon, and K. F. Powell. "Wishing with Dice," *Journal of Experimental Psychology*, L (1955), 269–275.

Murphy, G., and L. A. Dale. *Challenge of Psychical Research*. New York: Harper & Row, 1961.

Price, G. R. "Science and the Supernatural," *Science*, CXXII (1955), 359–367.

Sinclair, U. *Mental Radio*. Springfield, Ill.: Charles C Thomas, 1962.

Soal, S. G., and F. Bateman. *Modern Experiments in Telepathy*. London: Faber & Faber, 1954.

Soal, S. G., J. B. Rhine, P. E. Meehl, M. Scriven, P. W. Bridgman, G. R. Price, J. B. Rhine. (Letters to the editor in rejoinder to G. R. Price.) *Science*, CXXIII (1956), 9–19.

Stevens, S. S. "The Market for Miracles," *Contemporary Psychology*, XII (1967), 1–3.

THE SALE OF OCCULT BOOKS*

It has been suggested that a joint five-year educational objective of the American Society for Psychical Research and the Parapsychological Association should be to establish parapsychology as a normal topic for discussion in high schools and colleges throughout the United States.

Unthinkable even a few years ago, this is now a reasonable objective, brought within reach by recent developments (including the admission of the Parapsychological Association to affiliation with the American Association for the Advancement of Science). It has been estimated that five years would be needed for the completion of this project because of the unavoidable lag in preparing and introducing revised textbook editions but that 75 percent success could be attained within the next two years.

There are at present at least eight textbooks of general psychology giving favorable attention to ESP and, in some cases, to psychokinesis as

* Adapted from an article by R. A. McConnell and Tron McConnell, "Occult Books at the University of Pittsburgh," *Journal of the American Society for Psychical Research,* Vol. LXV, No. 3 (July 1971). I have retained the first-person-plural to acknowledge the collaboration of my son in the compilation of the statistical data. (Copyright 1971 by the American Society for Psychical Research, Inc.; copyright 1971 by R. A. McConnell.)

well. In this developing trend the role of the parapsychologists and their friends would be to provide systematic encouragement to those textbook authors who are not yet aware of the evidential status of these phenomena and of the widespread student demand for the forthright classroom examination of that status. It is expected that both the lay and professional psychical research organizations in this country will establish *ad hoc* committees for this objective. The members of the A.S.P.R. in particular, because they number over 2,000 and are widely dispersed, can play a key part in generating interest in the secondary schools.

There is reason to hope that the introduction of parapsychology, especially at the precollege level, before students have acquired an anti-intellectual bias, will provide sociotherapy by restoring the mystery of man's destiny to its proper inspirational role. At the same time this demonstration of orthodoxy's willingness to face the unknown may strengthen the faith of our young in science as an ennobling enterprise.

As a part of this eduacational project we present this study of the sale of books on occult subjects at a typical United States university. We think it is necessary to know and to understand the body of popular belief with which scientific parapsychology must contend and compete. Much of the reluctance of orthodox scientists to endorse expanded support for ESP research arises from their failure (and that of the lay press) to make a clear distinction between popular and scientific belief. We hope that this study will help make that difference plain.

Definition of "Occult Books"

"Occult books" we define as those dealing with psychological relationships whose reality, as manifest, is accepted by a sizable group of adults but denied or ignored in the orthodox belief systems of the prevailing culture.

From the occult category this definition excludes books on legerdemain, science fiction, health seeking, and hypnosis generally. (We have retained self-hypnosis as an occult subcategory because most such books contain ideas that go beyond orthodox teaching.)

Books on "unidentified flying objects" are borderline to our definition in that they may or may not postulate psychological relationships (with or between intelligent celestial beings). In any case, because of the quasi-technical nature of their readers' interests, these books have been grouped apart from the others.

Parapsychological books are "occult" under our definition because their claims are still widely ignored by the psychological profession. Five years from now this may no longer be true.

Classification of Occult Books

For present purposes we have devised the following ten-category classification scheme for occult books:

1. Celebrated psychics. (Books by or about individuals who purportedly had or have unusual psychic ability.)

2. Mysticism. (Books of ostensibly altruistic intent, encouraging unorthodox spiritual or general psychological self-development. Excluding books by or about outstanding psychics. Including yoga, Theosophy, Scientology, faith healing, self-hypnosis. No stories.)

3. Life after death. (Unorthodox books intended to convince rather than to titillate. Including spiritualism, reincarnation, and out-of-body experiences.)

4. Astrology. (Including its history.)

5. Other applied prediction and discovery. (How to develop or employ specific, useful occult powers, as by crystal gazing, dream interpretation, numerology, palmistry, handwriting analysis, phrenology, dowsing, clairvoyance, extrasensory perception.)

6. Black magic. (History of, and how to do it. Witchcraft, Satanism, voodoo, charms. No stories.)

7. Tales. (Occult legends, reports of bizarre natural events, excluding those about unidentified flying objects. Ghost, witch, and horror stories, including all works of ostensible fiction.)

8. Unidentified flying objects. ("Flying saucers.")

9. Parapsychology. (Presumptively scientific or scholarly works about psychic phenomena, or books that to a substantial degree treat scientific or scholarly research in this area, without regard to the merit of the treatment.)

10. Debunking. (Books whose purpose is to discredit some or all occult phenomena.)

Many of the classic works of the occult literature encountered in this survey were categorized from first- or secondhand knowledge of their content. About half of all books could be correctly placed with near certainty from the wording of the title or the name of the author. Certain distinctions (as between magic and stories involving magic) usually required actual inspection of the text. About 30 percent of all titles were inspected. Where uncertainty existed and where the book could not be found, a guess was made from title, author, publisher, and price. All classifications were made by the author who estimates his errors at less than 5 percent.

Source of the Data

The data of this study relate to books inventoried under the word "occult" at the University of Pittsburgh Book Center. With the exception of store inventory errors, all titles fitted into the classification scheme given above.

More specifically, we have dealt with those titles that were ordered from publishers in the one-year period August 1969 through July 1970. Because of limited inventory information, net sales could not be calculated.

In our original paper we discussed several reasons why the number of books ordered by this store might not accurately reflect the number of books sold to its customers in the same year. We concluded that our data represent sales for the given year to within perhaps 20 percent of the number in each category.

The University of Pittsburgh Book Center is a single, institutionally owned store, located in the heart of the campus on the main street of the cultural center of Pittsburgh. It handles all of the university's textbook needs on this campus except for medical books. The book center grossed $2.6 million in the 1969–70 fiscal year, of which amount 54 percent was in textbooks, 30 percent in trade books (including fine arts) and 16 percent in miscellaneous supplies. Forty-eight lineal feet of shelving were devoted to occult books.*

There are 2,000 college stores in the United States grossing $600 million. Of these, 125 take in more than $1 million a year. For college stores generally, 50 percent is a typical fraction of income from textbooks, and the average trade-book fraction is close to 10 percent. Although the last figure is lower than the corresponding figure for the University of Pittsburgh, we have some evidence suggesting that the nationwide ratio of occult-shelf-space to college-store-gross-sales is not far from the Pittsburgh value.

Who buys at this book center? Surveys by the store management have shown that 90 percent of the customers are university affiliated (faculty, students, subprofessional staff, or alumni) .

* Compared, for example, with religion (72 feet), travel (75 feet), and psychology, including personal guides and child care (175 feet) .

Who buys occult books? Not university faculty, or university graduate students, or students of the School of Engineering. Most of the patrons of the occult-book section we believe to be full-time, undergraduate students of the College of Arts and Sciences. These numbered 7,000 in each of the fall and winter terms of 1969–70. Unknown are the occult proclivities of the undergraduates in education (800), nursing (450), pharmacy (200), and night school (5,000). The total student enrollment in all categories at the Pittsburgh campus in each of these terms was 24,000.

We believe that our data fairly represent the magnitude and nature of the buying interest in occult books within the middle-class population served by this store. We are unable, however, to break down the sales between students and area residents. To make such a separation would require another study—which we hope will be done by some student parapsychological association on a more isolated campus, where college-store sales are restricted to staff and students.

Books in Each Category

In Table I (page 94) we present the number of titles, number of copies, and gross retail dollar value for paperback and clothbound books in each occult classification as ordered from publishers by this store in one year. The first six categories have been subtotaled separately for reasons that will now be explained.

The motivations of the buyers of occult books are diverse and complex. As parapsychologists, we are especially concerned with belief as a factor in buyer motivation. This matter might be approached by the quantitative methods of psychology, but for present purposes an intuitive analysis will suffice.

We have chosen to distinguish several kinds and degrees of belief in occult phenomena, namely: supernatural belief, fiction-science belief, scientific belief, unbelief, and disbelief.

"Supernatural belief" concerns nonphysical beings or powers derived from such. Mysticism, for example, usually involves at least tacit supernatural belief.

"Fiction-science belief" is an unsophisticated, unorthodox interpretation of strange phenomena under the assumption that they are part of three-dimensional reality still unknown to science. A belief in "flying saucers" falls into this category.

"Scientific belief" in occult phenomena, on the other hand, subjects itself to the methodological discipline of Western science but sets no preconditions on the "dimensionality" of the phenomena in question. Parapsychologists endeavor to discover the scientifically believable.

"Unbelief" is typified by the tolerant, uninterested stance toward occult phenomena adopted by most educated members of our culture. It is thought to be a defense mechanism against the anxiety that initially ensues when

occult phenomena are given serious considera-
tion.

"Disbelief" is a positive position indicating
emotional involvement. Authors of "debunking"
books are strongly motivated—perhaps by unconscious fear of the unknown mental entities
they are attempting to exorcise in others. The
authors of such books perhaps themselves believe
they are energized by love of truth or hatred
of error.

The reading of occult books is sometimes
solely for entertainment—in the same sense that
science-fiction books are commonly read without
belief. Without attempting an analysis of the distinction between the make-believe of fiction and
actual belief that persists and affects other behavior, we can safely say that many readers experience some degree of both kinds of belief
simultaneously, and that, for the same book, the
ratio of make-believe to actual belief varies from
reader to reader.

In the first six categories of Table I (covering
close to 70 percent of the surveyed books) we
presume that there is a large and usually domi-
nant degree of supernatural belief motivating
most purchases. These categories comprise what
might be called "hard-core occultism." They contain books that, as a rule, lack the redeeming
entertainment value of a plot. It is our opinion
that few store patrons will buy such books unless
they accept, or are ready to accept, the author's
message at face value. A few histories of witch-

craft and biographies of psychics are, in fact, scholarly works, but even these are sold primarily to readers whose interest is in the supernatural.

Another interesting breakdown is between the first three categories (books devoted to spiritual uplift) and the second three (books catering to a desire for personal power). Three times as much money is spent for power books as for uplift books—a disappointing commentary on Rousseau's idea that people tend naturally toward goodness.*

"Tales" (amounting to about 25 percent of occult books) have not been included in our hard-core group because we are unable to estimate to what extent they are taken seriously by their readers, or even, in many instances, whether their authors regarded them as truthful. Ghost stories, for example, almost always claim

---

* A statistical survey loses some of the flavor of its subject. Those who have not had occasion to browse through occult bookshelves may find something of interest among the following titles: *Astrology for Everyday Living. How to Put the Stars to Work for You. Astrology and the Single Girl. Astrology Made Easy. How to Meet and Keep Your Man Through Astrology. Lunar Cycle in Relation to Human Conception and Sex of Offspring. ESP and the Stars. Palmistry for Pleasure and Profit. Handwriting Analysis for Teens. The Complete Gypsy Fortune Teller. Nature's Symphony, or Lessons in Number Vibrations. Power Through Witchcraft. Practical Candle Burning. Sex and Satanism. More Ghosts in Irish Houses. Vampires, Werewolves, and Ghouls. The Lost Continent of Mu. The Bible and Flying Saucers. Flying Saucers—Serious Business. Unidentified Aquatic Objects.*

to be historical accounts and often provide much "corroborative detail intended to give artistic verisimilitude to an otherwise bald and unconvincing narrative."

On the other hand, this category includes some well-authenticated case histories of unexplained events, which, according to one's judgment, might instead have been called parapsychological.

The small number (3 percent) of titles fulfilling even our liberal definition of "parapsychological" reflects the status of this pretheoretical science, struggling to emerge from a morass of uncritical belief.

The still smaller number of debunking books (two-tenths of 1 percent) results, we believe, from two factors. It is no longer possible to make a credible case against parapsychology, and there is no market for "negative thinking" books.

In our journal paper, *loc. cit.,* we examined our data to determine how many and what kinds of publishers were selling occult books, and we validated our findings by a comparison with the publishers of 598 books listed under "Occult Sciences" in a recent issue of *Paperbound Books in Print.* The 454 clothbound and paperback titles of Table I came from 67 publishers, 37 of whom had only one or two titles. The largest number of books from a single publisher was 64, half of which were in astrology and one-third in "other applied prediction and discovery." Together these made up one-third of all books in these categories—a surprising concentration.

TABLE I | OCCULT BOOKS BY SUBJECT CLASSIFICATION

Purchased by the University of Pittsburgh Book Center in the period August 1969 through July 1970. Except for rounding, all columns total 100 percent. Absolute values can be obtained by multiplying cell entry by column heading.

	TITLES			COPIES			RETAIL VALUE		
N or $	Paper 345	Cloth 109	Total 454	Paper 3488	Cloth 550	Total 4038	Paper $3704	Cloth $3475	Total $7179
Noted psychics	9%	13%	10%	11%	11%	11%	10%	11%	10%
Mysticism	2	9	4	2	4	2	2	4	3
Life after death	5	6	6	7	8	7	5	4	5
Astrology	21	22	21	22	29	24	20	31	25
Other prediction	17	9	15	16	14	16	22	16	19
Black magic	11	10	11	12	8	11	17	9	13
Subtotal (Supernatural belief)	65%	69%	67%	70%	74%	71%	76%	75%	75%
Tales	28	23	27	25	20	24	19	20	20
UFOs	3	4	3	3	2	2	2	2	2
Parapsychology	4	3	3	2	3	3	3	3	3
Debunking	0.3	0.9	0.4	0.1	0.9	0.2	0.1	0.6	0.4

HOW TO CONDUCT AN ESP
PICTURE-DRAWING
EXPERIMENT

The following procedure is complex. Perhaps
you can devise a simpler but equally foolproof
method. If your only purpose is to demonstrate
probable ESP without actually "proving" it,
many of the precautions can be relaxed. But in
such cases the loopholes you leave should be
discussed by the class before or after the experiment.

In addition to the experimenter and student
subjects, the given procedure calls for an "outsider" to perform certain test functions. The
judging of success may be done by anyone except
the outsider, or it may be done by the consensus
of a group.

1. From magazines and other sources secretly
gather a large number of target pictures, selected
for distinctiveness, strong lines, striking content.
Mark on each picture a code number consisting
of T followed by identifying digits.

2. Choose the needed number of target pictures and place them individually between sheets
of aluminum foil. Put each such sandwich inside
an adhesive-flap manila envelope, and seal it.
This step should be done by the outsider.

3. Code each target envelope on its outside
by an R followed by digits that are unrelated to

the T digits inside. Avoid marking through onto the target. This step should be done by the experimenter, who, for the time being, must remain in ignorance of the pictures within the envelopes lest he unwittingly give a clue to the subjects.

4. Place each target-containing envelope under glass within a suitable holding frame so that the R-code is showing. The purpose of the glass is to prevent a subject from accidentally pressure-marking the target picture when making his response drawing.

5. Tape to the surface of the glass one edge of blank drawing paper bearing the same R-code number that is visible on the envelope.

6. Psychologically prepare the student subjects.

7. Distribute one "target-response assembly" (picture holder, etc.) to each student and maintain under surveillance until collected.

8. Have each student draw his impression of his target on the blank paper.

9. Collect the target-response assemblies and store safely.

10. In order to score the results, you must arrange the target-response assemblies in easy-to-manage groups of, say, four to ten. This may be done randomly or by intuitive or quantitative criteria. For example, it may be done on the basis of the response drawings themselves or on the basis of some characteristic of the persons who made the drawings, such as sex, personality

trait, academic ability, or previous performance on an ESP experiment. (See below.)

11. For each group of target-response assemblies have the/an outsider open and record T number versus R number for each assembly. He should then lay aside the empty envelopes, shuffle the target pictures, and shuffle the response drawings. (If desired, the response drawings may be removed from the assemblies by someone else before this step, since the R number is also on the envelope under the glass.)

12. Give each group of shuffled targets and the corresponding shuffled responses to the judge to match. He must choose one response drawing to go with each target picture, using whatever criteria may have been agreed upon. He should report his results as a list of pairs of T and R numbers.

13. A comparison of the judge's list of T-R number pairs with the list of true pairs obtained in Step 11 will show every judge's pair to be a hit or a mismatch. At least a few hits are expected to occur merely by chance. The probability of obtaining by chance as many hits or matches as were actually obtained in any group is found in the following table.

14. Combine the probabilities of all groups by the method described below.

15. You may wish to bring to class the targets and corresponding responses for inspection and discussion.

The workings of the statistical method are such that the final combined probability for the experiment as a whole will be smaller if the judging groups are large and if the better responses can somehow be grouped together in Step 10, i.e., if impossible-to-match pairs can be segregated by some legitimate procedure. Moreover (by mathematical methods not included in this guide), it may be possible to decide whether one group showed significantly more ESP than another.

The requirement of "legitimacy" in the grouping of the responses (by other than a random process) will be met if the targets remain concealed and unknown to the person doing the grouping until he has finished that task.

It is also allowable to group target-response pairs on the basis of the kinds of targets used if the grouping is done by the outsider without knowledge of the response drawings.

The probabilities associated with several groups of target-response pictures (whether of the same size or not) may be combined into a single probability by the following method. From a table of probabilities of the "normal curve of error" giving the area under the two tails of the curve versus the "standard score" (i.e., the Critical Ratio or x/σ) find the standard score corresponding to each group probability. (If the table gives one-tail versus standard score, enter the table with one-half of the group probability.) The sum of the squares of the resulting standard scores is a "chi-square" with "degrees of freedom" equal to the number of groups. The desired combined probability is found from a table of chi-squares. Normal dis-

CUMULATIVE PROBABILITIES FOR MATCHING PAIRS

The probability of making r, or more, correct matches in the random pairing of n targets with n responses. (The notation 1.98–4 means 0.000198.)

r	n = 3	4	5	6	7	8	9	10
1	.667	.625	.633	.632	.632	.632	.632	.632
2	—	.292	.258	.265	.264	.264	.264	.264
3	.167	—	.0917	.0778	.0808	.0802	.0803	.0803
4		.0417	—	.0222	.01825	.01912	.01897	.01899
5			.00833	—	.00436	.00350	.00369	.00366
6				.00139	—	7.19–4	5.65–4	6.00–4
7					1.98–4	—	1.02–4	7.88–5
8						2.48–5	—	1.27–5
9							2.76–6	—
10								2.76–7

tribution and chi-square tables are in textbooks of statistical method and in various handbooks, such as the Chemical Rubber Company *Handbook of Chemistry and Physics*.

Needless to say, *all* of the probabilities, large or small, obtained in a particular experiment or group of experiments must be included when finding an over-all chance probability, and the basis for putting the data together must be stated along with the probability. Otherwise the procedure will be misleading.

Often the above method of analysis does not do justice to individual successes. The subjects with the most dramatic successes might be selected for further experiments.

HOW TO CONDUCT A CARD-
GUESSING EXPERIMENT

The test procedure to be described uses an ordinary playing-card deck and is perhaps the simplest of possible ways to look for ESP in the classroom.

Because novelty is an important element in producing ESP, "preliminary" tests when using groups of unselected students should be avoided. This means that advance planning is necessary.

Preparing the Targets

Remove from the playing-card deck the jacks, queens, and kings, leaving 40 cards, in which the aces are to be regarded as ones.

Before coming to class the instructor should shuffle the cards and place one in each of 40 opaque card-size envelopes. These could be sealed; but if the cards are inserted face toward the flap side, merely turning in the flap should be enough to prevent accidental recognition. After the envelopes have been filled they should be shuffled. A further final cut or shuffle just before use is advisable.

Because envelopes may have visible differences that could give unwitting cues, for absolute safety they should be filled by a responsible person who will not be present during the experiment. In laboratory research double envelopes are often used. Although these precautions are unnecessary for most classroom work, care must be taken that the envelopes are not handled by the students who will guess them.

Preparing the Data Sheets

Even for informal testing it is generally necessary to prepare the data-recording sheets in advance. Otherwise a few students will fail to follow instructions when recording their data, and the resulting uncertainties in the statistical evaluation will obscure the meaning of the experiment.

The data sheets for this kind of experiment might consist of mimeographed half-size pages with a heading for name, class, and date above a group of four column-boxes, which are subdivided into ten rows each. Suggested dimensions for the column-boxes are $3/4$-inch width and $3/4$-inch separation. The cell height within the boxes can be $3/8$ inches, making the over-all height $33/4$ inches. This will allow room for one or two symbols in each cell. Wide margins and the space between boxes will be useful for scoring.

Each data page should be stapled on one edge to a carbon sheet and a blank page of the same size. After the card guessing is completed, the instructor will ask each student to separate the sheets and to pass in the original and the carbon paper, while keeping the carbon copy for immediate scoring.

Making the Guesses

Although everyone is familiar with playing cards, you should have a spare deck as a visual aid when explaining the test procedure.

After the class has been given instructions and aroused to an appropriate degree of enthusiasm, the instructor or a student delegate, starting with the 40 target envelopes in one pile, will hold them up, one at a time, and, after the students have recorded their guesses, lay them down in a second pile in a box that will prevent them from sliding out of order. The timing and other details of procedure can be varied according to the purpose and intuition of the experimenter but should be thought about in advance and described in the plan of the experiment. One specific suggestion seems worth making at this point. For most ESP experimental purposes, 40 card guesses are too many to make without interruption. A few moments' rest with a word or two by the instructor should be given at the end of each column of ten guesses.

Scoring the Results

The students may have been instructed to guess at the face number of the card $(p = \frac{1}{10})$ or at its suit $(p = \frac{1}{4})$ or at both. The scoring and statistical evaluation will, of course, be different in these cases. A table is included herewith from which one may find the chance probability of any one student getting a score equal to or higher than the one actually obtained.

After the guessing is done and the original sheet and carbon paper have been collected and placed in a prepared envelope for future use, the classroom scoring should be carried out. Promptly learning their results is important for the satisfaction and continuing interest of the students.

The pile of the target cards in envelopes should be turned over and the envelopes opened one at a time in the order of their original presentation. As the cards are removed they should be held up and, depending upon the plan of the experiment, the number or suit or both should be called out so that the students can mark their carbon-copy records to show correct guesses.

At the same time the instructor should record on a prepared data sheet (with carbon) the true order of the target cards for later independent checking of the student original sheets. Enough time should be allowed in opening the envelopes so that the students can keep in step and so that the master record by the instructor is accurate.

When the scoring is finished and the hits of whatever kinds have been totaled by each student, the various numbers of successes that occurred in the class can be tabulated on the chalk board and the probabilities explained.

At some point prior to the end of the discussion the students' carbon records should also be collected. These can be useful in verifying the independent scoring and lend themselves to interesting studies of student accuracy.

Miscellaneous Suggestions for This and Similar Experiments

The discussion between experimenter and subjects preceding the actual card guessing is undoubtedly the most important part of the experiment, although we cannot specify exactly how it should be done. The mechanical procedures that will be followed must be carefully explained to avoid anxiety as well as mistakes. But most of all, at this stage the experimenter must develop in the entire group a sense of freedom, enthusiasm, and confidence.

Among other things, the subjects may be told that their success at card guessing does not require having had previous psychic experiences. Contrary to popular supposition, card guessing is too specialized and artificial to be a good test for spontaneous psychic tendencies.

For rigorous testing, card shuffling by hand is satisfactory if done by interleaving riffles rather than by shoving. (This avoids the possibility that somewhat similar cards may tend to cumulate together.) The final cut should be done by fingernail or knife rather than by allowing the deck to fall apart. (High cards, having more ink, may tend to stick together.)

The cards must be entirely concealed from the subjects who are doing the guessing. If the test is one in which the cards are not actually

CUMULATIVE BINOMIAL PROBABILITIES FOR 40 TRIALS

Chance probability of getting at least (or no more than) r correct guesses for trial probability, p.

(The notation 1.33-4 means 0.000133. Parenthetical probabilities are for "no more than.")

r	p = 1/2	1/3	1/4	1/5	1/10	1/40
0	(9.1-13)	(9.04-8)	(1.01-5)	(1.33-4)	(.01478)	(.36323)
1	(3.7-11)	(1.90-6)	(1.44-4)	(.00146)	(.08047)	.63677
2	(7.5-10)	(1.95-5)	(.00102)	(.00794)	(.22281)	.26422
3	(9.73-9)	(1.31-4)	(.00470)	(.02846)	(.42313)	.07795
4	(9.29-8)	(6.48-4)	(.01604)	(.07591)	.57687	.01745
5	(6.91-7)	(.00251)	(.04327)	(.16133)	.37098	.00310
6	(4.18-6)	(.00793)	(.09622)	(.28589)	.20627	4.51-4
7	(2.11-5)	(.02110)	(.18195)	(.43715)	.09952	5.51-5
8	(9.11-5)	(.04827)	(.29983)	.56285	.04190	5.74-6
9	(3.40-4)	(.09657)	(.43954)	.40687	.01550	5.16-7
10	(.00111)	(.17144)	.56046	.26822	.00506	4.06-8
11	(.00321)	(.27352)	.41610	.16077	.00147	2.82-9
12	(.00829)	(.39688)	.28486	.08751	3.81-4	1.7-10
13	(.01924)	(.52972)	.17913	.04324	8.84-5	9.5-12
14	(.04035)	.47028	.10323	.01941	1.85-5	4.7-13
15	(.07693)	.34218	.05444	.00792	3.48-6	2.1-14
16	(.13409)	.23116	.02624	.00294	5.93-7	8.3-16

17	(.21480)	.14443	.01156	9.91-4	9.14-8	3.0-17
18	(.31791)	.08320	.00465	3.04-4	1.28-8	9.7-19
19	(.43731)	.04409	.00171	8.52-5	1.62-9	2.9-20
20	.56269	.02144	5.72-4	2.17-5	1.9-10	7.7-22
21	.48731	.00955	1.75-4	5.08-6	2.0-11	1.9-23
22	.31791	.00389	4.86-5	1.06-6	1.9-12	4.2-25
23	.21480	.00145	1.23-5	2.03-7	1.6-13	8.4-27
24	.13409	4.89-4	2.83-6	3.52-8	1.3-14	1.5-28
25	.07693	1.50-4	5.88-7	5.53-9	8.8-16	2.5-30
26	.04035	4.17-5	1.11-7	7.9-10	5.6-17	3.7-32
27	.01924	1.05-5	1.87-8	1.0-10	3.2-18	4.9-34
28	.00829	2.36-6	2.84-9	1.1-11	1.7-19	5.8-36
29	.00321	4.74-7	3.9-10	1.1-12	7.6-21	6.1-38
30	.00111	8.47-8	4.6-11	1.1-13	3.1-22	5.8-40
31	3.40-4	1.34-8	4.9-12	8.5-15	1.1-23	4.8-42
32	9.11-5	1.84-9	4.5-13	5.9-16	3.4-25	3.4-44
33	2.11-5	2.2-10	3.6-14	3.5-17	9.1-27	2.1-46
34	4.18-6	2.2-11	2.5-15	1.8-18	2.1-28	1.1-48
35	6.91-7	1.9-12	1.4-16	7.7-20	3.9-30	4.9-51
36	9.29-8	1.3-13	6.3-18	2.6-21	6.1-32	1.8-53
37	9.73-9	6.8-15	2.3-19	7.1-23	7.3-34	4.9-56
38	7.5-10	2.6-16	5.9-21	1.4-24	6.4-36	9.8-59
39	3.7-11	6.7-18	1.0-22	1.8-26	3.6-38	1.3-61
40	9.1-13	8.2-20	8.3-25	1.1-28	1.0-40	8.3-65

enclosed, revealing reflections from polished surfaces must be avoided.

Anyone who knows the card order must remain silent during the guessing period or, better yet, be in another room to avoid the possibility of unconsciously giving clues.

If observers or witnesses must be present, they should be placed so they cannot give cues to the subjects, and preferably should be given some incidental task that makes them a part of the experiment. This minimizes the danger of embarrassing or distracting the subjects.

If the usual card deck with a definite number of cards of each kind is used, subjects must not learn of any success or failure in guessing until they have reached the end of the deck. (If the targets are derived from a "random number table," this precaution is unnecessary.)

There are other minor disadvantages in the use of a deck of a fixed composition. To the extent that the guesser adjusts his guessing to avoid too many or too few repetitions, the successive pairs of guess-versus-target are not entirely independent, and a slight bias will arise in calculating the "standard deviation" needed to test the null hypothesis.

Of more real importance is the danger that a subject's attempts to "use up the right number of guesses" will distract him and inhibit ESP. It is well for this reason to instruct subjects to pay no attention to the guesses they have already made but to think of each card as though it were not part of a deck.

The record of card-order and guess-order

should be written down separately on separate sheets of paper and brought together for the checking. If a single sheet is used, the guess column must be covered when the targets are being recorded. If the target order is copied while the guesses are visible, there is a very real danger that the person doing the copying will unconsciously write down a wrong target to match the visible guess. The possibility of even infrequent errors of this kind will make the data worthless for evidential purposes.

The probabilities obtained by scoring separately for card number and for suit can be combined into a single probability by the method given in the appendix describing a picture-drawing experiment, or by the use of the furnished table for $p = \frac{1}{40}$. For the latter, a card yields one correct guess only if both number *and* suit are correctly named.

If the test is one in which a group is guessing and you expect to combine individual scores to obtain a group probability, it is preferable that each person be aiming at his own separate set of targets. Otherwise there may be a tendency for subjects to guess alike, and this might bias the probability calculation.

A specific example may make this clear. Suppose the class has just seen a movie on diamond mining and as a result their guesses on the first card are predominantly diamonds. Under these circumstances if a diamond card is the target, an unusual number of hits would occur. Conversely, if the target is not a diamond, a deficit of hits could result. The average expected score would not be altered, but the fluctuation in score would be wider than usual. Consequently, the "standard deviation" used for evaluating the departure of the obtained score from the expected average would be too small and the chance probability would be underestimated.

With ordinary precautions against conversation, in a class of 50 or fewer students guessing at the same card deck, this effect should be negligibly small. Just how small is an interesting question on which little research has been done.

To avoid fatigue, experiments and experimental sessions should be kept short. Twenty-five to fifty guesses in a session is generally the maximum. Fewer may be better.

The length of the experiment should be determined in advance. A slight, indefinite bias is introduced if the decision to end the experiment is based in part upon the success so far achieved.

All data gathered in whatever has been designated in advance as a particular experiment must be used in the final evaluation. If the records of poor results are lost or omitted, the remainder will falsely tend to appear better than chance.

The person or persons in charge of the experiment should handle the cards, make the written records during checkup, and in every way satisfy themselves that the research plan is being followed and all precautions are being observed. Responsibility in a scientific experiment of this kind cannot be delegated to untrained or uninformed helpers if dependable results are wanted.

BUILDING A PK PLACEMENT APPARATUS

Construct a reasonably flat tabletop, say 80 × 100 cm, with 10 cm or taller edge fences to keep the dice in. Stretch a steel wire, say of 1 mm diameter, down the middle, in the long direction, flat against the table surface, with provision for keeping it taut and in a constant position. Dice that come to rest on this division wire will tip to one side or the other and are to be scored accordingly.

The tabletop might be the rough side of either "tempered" or soft fiberboard, chosen to allow free but erratic tumbling of cubes along its surface.

Build a die-releasing mechanism, operated by an electromagnet actuated by a push button at the end of a loosely draped wire. The releasing mechanism should hold six cubes of the chosen size (say ⅝″ on an edge) in a definite position. When actuated, the releasing mechanism should drop or slide the cubes onto an inclined plane, sloping down at perhaps 45 degrees toward an edge of the table that is bisected by the division wire. The releasing mechanism and inclined plane should be centered on the axis of the division wire so that the released cubes tend to come to rest in approximately equal numbers on the two sides of the wire.

Label the two halves of the tabletop *A* and *B*. The actual chance probability of getting the cubes into halves *A* and *B* can be estimated by lumping the results of all cubes in an experiment without regard to wishing. The exact probability value is not important, but it can be expected to lie between 0.4 and 0.6, and it must be *constant* insofar as it is determined by the mechanical setup.

The floor must be firm. The table must not wobble. The entire mechanism must be rigidly constructed. The moving parts of the releasing mechanism should have minimum practical play. Slight random fluctuations in bias toward one side or the other will be of no consequence, but controllable, mechanical bias that might associate with the wishing will destroy the value of the experiment.

For further constructional ideas you may wish to study a paper that appeared in the *Journal of Parapsychology*, XXXII (1968), 9–38, as well as earlier papers referred to therein.

There are any number of possible releasing-mechanism designs. The choice of materials and geometry should be such that the cubes descend with jumping, random motions. The more lively they appear, the better.

To perform a PK placement experiment, prepare a plan and make up data sheets for a procedure such as the following:

Place six plastic or unpainted-wood (i.e., non-sticky) cubes in the release mechanism. In some of the most careful experiments these have been numbered and placed with a standard order and orientation. For exploratory work it suffices to place the cubes randomly, providing that as a group they are snugly together and occupy the same definite position before each release.

A typical plan might call for the cubes to be released 5 successive times (by one person) while wishing them to come to Side *A*, followed by 5 times wishing for Side *B*. This might constitute a single test session. (The test sessions must be kept short.) The next day the procedure should be reversed: 5 releases for Side *B* followed by 5 for *A*. And so on, for a total of perhaps six sessions.

From a purely mechanical viewpoint it might be thought best to change targets after each release, but there is evidence that the psychological adjustment requires time and must not be too frequently attempted.

Great care must be taken in reading the cubes. Duplicate, independent records, one by the "test subject" and one by a friendly observer, should be kept. The number of cubes on Side *A* should be silently counted and recorded; after which the cubes on Side *B* should be counted and recorded. The two recorders should next compare records. *Only then should the cubes be touched.*

The results are most easily evaluated by what is called a "chi-square contingency test" using a desk calculator or logarithms. The raw data consist of four numbers, a, b, c, d, representing how many cubes appeared on the two sides of the table for each of the specified wishing conditions (i.e., for Side *A* and for Side *B*). These numbers may be entered in a 2-by-2 array and the edge and corner frequencies figured by addition as shown in the diagram herewith. You will notice that *a* and *d* are the numbers of cubes behaving as desired, while *b* and *c* represent the number of cubes that went the wrong ways.

Wished to
go to side

Actually
went
to side

	A	B	
A	a	b	a + b
B	c	d	c + d
	a + c	b + d	n

where n = a + b + c + d

The square of the "critical ratio" is calculated from the following formula:

$$(CR)^2 = \frac{n\,(|ad - bc| - n/2)^2}{(a+b)\,(c+d)\,(a+c)\,(b+d)}$$

The CR, sometimes symbolized by z, is a standard score on the "normal distribution," for which probability tables are readily available.

This method of analysis assumes that the six cubes behave independently, and, in particular, that the cubes do not tend for mechanical reasons to travel as a group to one side or the other. In most apparatus constructions this effect is negligible or the opposite tendency predominates, so that the binomial assumption gives a conservative test. In advanced research this question might be investigated by an "analysis of variance" using the measured final resting positions of numbered cubes.

Please send information to
 Prof. R. A. McConnell
 Biophysics & Microbiology Dept.
 University of Pittsburgh
 Pittsburgh, Pa. 15213

Today's date:

Instructor's name:

Name and mailing address of school:

Name and mailing address of instructor (if different from school) :

In what course was the ESP curriculum guide used?

When were the course and unit given?

Please give the author, title, edition, and publisher of the text you used in the course.

How many class hours were devoted to this topic?

Approximately how many students took the course?

Suggestions for improving the curriculum guide or any other comment you care to offer:

Would you care to describe any ESP or PK experiments conducted by your students? If a report was prepared, a copy would be appreciated.

INDEXES

INDEX OF NAMES

SUBJECT INDEX